'I have to come up with a sermon ...'

In God alone is my soul at rest (Ps 61)

Fr Mark Hartley O.C.S.O.

'I have to come up with a sermon ...'

Year A

the columba press

First published in 2013 by
the columba press
55A Spruce Avenue, Stillorgan Industrial Park,
Blackrock, Co. Dublin

Cover by Shaun Gallagher
Images courtesy of Mount Saint Bernard Abbey, Leicester
Origination by The Columba Press
Printed by ScandBook, Sweden

ISBN 978 1 78218 083 8

Acknowledgements

Many thanks to Fr Joseph Delargy, Fr Hilary Costello, John and Rosalind Hartley, Maureen Havers, Doris Hudson and Peter McFadyen for their help with this book. Thanks also to Michael Brennan and Patrick O'Donoghue from The Columba Press. Above all, thanks to Fr Mark Hartley for writing the sermons in the first place.

Nicola Roberts

Contents

Biographies

Fr Mark Hartley o.c.s.o.
Fr Mark was a monk at Mount Saint Bernard Abbey, Leicester, for fifty-six years. He was also Secretary of the Panel of Monastic Musicians, a national, ecumenical group of religious men and women. He died suddenly in 2010 from an inoperable brain tumour.

Editors

Maureen Havers
Maureen lives with her husband, John, on the abbey estate. Fr Mark was much loved by all their family since the 1970s. Maureen says that it is a privilege to re-hear his voice in these sermons.

Fr Hilary Costello o.c.s.o.
Fr Hilary entered Mount Saint Bernard Abbey a few years before Fr Mark and lived with him for nearly sixty years as a close friend. Hilary has contributed many articles and books about the Cistercian Fathers and similar subjects. He is currently working on the *Life of St Bernard*.

Nicola Roberts
Nicola is a fully qualified secretary/administrator and worked alongside Fr Mark throughout his ten years in the Monastery shop. She also helped him in his work for the Panel of Monastic Musicians. Nicola continues to enjoy looking after the shop alongside the monks.

Prologue

The homilies published in this book were preached by my brother, Fr Mark Hartley O.C.S.O., on various occasions during his life as a Cistercian monk of Mount Saint Bernard Abbey, Leicester. He was meticulous in preparing his sermons, and although he delivered them by reading the text, he did it in a way which came over not only as fluent and spontaneous, but also as sincere. His gentle, unflamboyant style appealed to many. But what was most appreciated was his ability, despite his apparent isolation in a monastery, to connect his spiritual insights with what was going on in the world. He kept abreast of current affairs and events, and had a genuine understanding of the lot of ordinary folk. He may not have been *in* the world but he was certainly *of* it. Having done two six-year stints as guestmaster at the abbey, he was acutely sensitive to the needs, concerns and problems that people encountered; and the wise advice and counsel he gave to thousands of visitors to the abbey over many years were greatly appreciated. He was always willing to give his time to people whatever the cost to himself.

Fr Mark's efficient filing systems and exceptional IT skills have served, among other things, to ensure that all 700 of his homilies given at the abbey and elsewhere were initially retained in print and later recorded on a memory stick – enabling the selection in this little book to be readily made. There is nothing extraordinary about the homilies in themselves; but since they were written by one person, in one place, over a period of fifty-six years, they reflect a harmony and continuity of thought and style which are quite remarkable.

John Hartley
Newcastle, Staffordshire

Introduction

The constitutions of the Cistercian Order, to which Fr Mark Hartley belonged for fifty-six years, state:

> The changing seasons of the liturgical year have great power to nourish and enrich the contemplative life of the brothers and sisters. They provide a solid basis for the preaching and teaching given to the community.
>
> (Const. 17.2)

These sixty-five sermons all stem from the seasons of the liturgical year or the feasts that occur during it. On the whole they were preached in three contexts: to the monastic community and assembled public congregation at the Sunday Eucharist, to the assembled public congregation at an earlier Sunday Eucharist or just to the monastic community assembled in the chapter house for an evening sermon on the eve of a great feast. The liturgical year was the solid basis for Fr Mark's teaching and preaching to the monastic community and to the Sunday congregations.

The Cistercian Fathers, those monks from the earliest years of the Order in the 12th century, did not seem to hesitate in making their sermons public; we think of the liturgical sermons of St Bernard of Clairvaux, Guerric of Igny and St Aelred of Rievaulx. Whilst no one would claim that Fr Mark's sermons are in the same category as those of these great men of the past, nevertheless the aim is the same, to hand on the fruits of his contemplation to a wider audience. I would like to thank Nicola Roberts for overseeing the compilation of this book, and The Columba Press for publishing it.

Fr Joseph Delargy
Mount Saint Bernard Abbey,
Easter 2013

The Mount Saint Bernard Abbey Community
Fr Mark – second row, third from right

SERMONS

Advent Promises

2nd Sunday of Advent (2004)

Have you noticed how the world, life in general, is governed by promises? Promises lure us on for they are the stuff of which dreams are made. Unfortunately, promises do not materialise overnight. School leavers who expect to be managing directors, pop stars, footballers, have to learn one of the most basic lessons of life: that success and prosperity do not come instantly or without a hard slog. People want the goods now, not promises. It's like that child who came home from school looking very unhappy. When his mother asked him what was the matter, he replied, 'The teacher said "wait there for the present". I waited and she never gave it me.'

Haven't we all had unfulfilled promises? Have you ever bought a gadget, believing all the ads promised about it, only to be sadly disappointed when it arrived? And to be further disappointed when the promise of money back proved to be hedged in by small print that prevented you getting your money back.

Disappointment and unfulfilled promises litter our lives and leave us rather cynical. What is perhaps even more worrying, we accuse others of failing to live up to their promises only to find ourselves desperately making excuses for our own failures to live up to what we have promised we would do ourselves. What about those resolutions, those things you have promised yourself you'll do, or have promised others? You get up in the morning and think to yourself: 'O yes, I must do this', 'go to confession, it's Advent!', 'visit so and so', 'pay that bill', 'sign up for that course'.

They talk about health warnings but loss of confidence in promises, both in our own and others, can seriously damage the health of our faith. When so many of the certainties of this life have failed to materialise it is easy to find ourselves beginning to doubt the very truths and promises of our faith. I suggest, if you get a minute sometime during the week, to take another look at today's readings. They are absolutely marvellous in their belief and assurance of the wonderful things to come when

God's kingdom arrives. Not just the promise of *things* either, but above all of *someone* to come. Baruch tells us about a shoot coming from the stock of Jesse and how the spirit of the Lord will be upon him. The psalm tells us more: 'In his days justice shall flourish.' In a world where inequality and injustice, war and strife are so widespread it is balm to hear of justice and peace flourishing when our Saviour comes.

It's there again in St Paul. It's in the gospel. John the Baptist himself echoes that divine promise when he proclaims that all humanity 'shall see the salvation of our God' (Lk 3:6).

Advent is all about readjusting our lenses. A good example is like driving on the motorway in rain. The windscreen soon gets covered with spray. Without regular use of the washer and wiper it would become impossible to see. Advent is like that; it's about looking again, through a clean windscreen, at our familiar surroundings and seeing them with fresh eyes. A friend of mine said she once forgot to fill the washer tank with water so when she pressed the button nothing happened. Nothing will happen in Advent without the water of faith. We've got to believe in a promise. But it is not the promise of a roaring lion; it is the promise of a bleating lamb.

If we believe in the promises of which the lessons this morning are so full, we could well find ourselves asking *how does God intend to implement them*, then? He sends a Saviour upon whom the spirit of the Lord rests, the spirit of wisdom and insight, the spirit of counsel and power. What this is telling us is not only about how life in the kingdom will be, but *how we should be*, as we are full members, brothers and sisters of Jesus through our baptism. *We* are the ones to implement the promises. Not only does the spirit rest upon Jesus, but that same spirit of wisdom and discernment, knowledge and fear of the Lord rests on us.

This is where Advent is so important. The world, like the lorries ahead of you on the motorway, is showering us with mud, and clouding our vision. As a result we let our trust in God's power to implement his promises slip from our grasp. Advent readings remind us of God's promises; they revive in us the hope we have of a Saviour, and stir up the grace of the Holy Spirit in us. Don't they call it Pudding Sunday because the opening words of the Collect were: STIR UP! (*Excita potentiam tuam, Domine, et veni.*) Gradually, once again, God's love comes and is born again in our souls. It's up to us to allow God to work this new birth in us. WE ARE THE PEOPLE OF THE PROMISE!

Advent Means Visitation

2ⁿᵈ Sunday of Advent (2007)

If you have ever visited a country house like Chatsworth (Derbyshire), one of the highlights of the house's history is always when a great monarch visited. Someone like Queen Elizabeth I or Queen Victoria. I remember at my old school, the memory of a reigning queen's visit was treasured long after the event. During Advent, we can see the significance of this when you realise that the Latin word *Adventus* can be translated as 'presence' or 'visitation'. It was used particularly for the visit of some high dignitary and especially for the arrival of kings.

It doesn't need me to say how this word became adopted by Christians in order to express their belief in the coming of their God among them. Christians believe their king has visited this wretched province Earth. Just like the great country houses, we continue to treasure the memory to this day. We may not have photos of the occasion but artists have pictured it times innumerable. Our God is not just like the Queen or Prime Minister, a VIP who seldom comes to unimportant places like here. Our God has done just that and, what is far more important, he still visits us in a thousand different ways.

A nun was telling the children in her class the story of the birth of Jesus. She began with Mary and Joseph coming along the road from Nazareth to Bethlehem. When they arrived, they tried the hotel but found it was booked out. The manager suggested a place up the road. They tried there too and it was the same story. A passer-by told them of a cave up the hillside. So they went there and found it had been used to house farm animals. It had no door; it was damp and dirty and cold. 'Now,' she asked the children, 'what would you have done if you had been there with them?' One little boy's hand shot up: 'Sister, I would have got a broom and swept the place clean.' A little girl said she would have made three cups of tea: one for Mary, one for Joseph and one for Jesus. A second little boy had his answer: 'I would have taken my jacket off and wrapped it around baby Jesus.' Another one was all for making a big fire. He was a Cub (junior member of the Scout Association) and knew about such things. Finally, a timid little girl put her hand up. 'Sister,' the little girl said in a whisper, 'if Mary would have let me, I would have taken the baby in my arms and just loved him.' That was the best answer of all. He came because he loved us and he wants our love before all else in return.

There are two points that this story brings out. First of all, it starts where my first example left off. My first example was of the visit of a famous person to an equally famous place. It is true of Jesus' visit: he is a very important person: he is the King of Kings, and Lord of Lords. We still celebrate and rejoice about his coming among us to this day. Like all examples, however, it limps because it suggests that Jesus is like earthly kings and only visits important people and stays in grand mansions.

That is where the other story puts the record straight. Jesus came among us as the least and the lowest; he started off, not in the palace of King Herod, but in a desolate cave outside Bethlehem. But, it too can give the wrong message because you can see how all the children wanted to *do* things for Jesus, *give* things to Jesus. That is a very praiseworthy aspect – our loving service. But what Jesus wants from us at Christmas is not more effort, more money. What he wants is more love. For us Catholics one of the best ways of doing that is making a very loving and well-prepared Confession and Holy Communion.

Coming back to our original idea of Advent meaning visit or visitation, I think the word *visit* opens up other possible kinds of visitation. We may have to be prepared for the Lord to visit us with the harder things in life. For some, illness and suffering may be how the Lord has visited you this Christmas. Even when it is difficult for us, we should at least try to understand the days of our illness in this way: the Lord has interrupted my doing, my sweeping, my cooking, my lighting a fire in order to let me be still and love him like the little girl.

If that is the way Advent is for you this year, how the Lord has visited you or your family, the other way is for you yourself to visit someone who is alone and ill. In this way, you yourself can be like Jesus and visit the sick and housebound. If it's tough being sick, it can require a lot of grace and goodwill to go and visit people who are ill.

So let us make this Advent a time when we ponder the different ways it can be a visitation of Jesus and the different ways we can respond to it. But above all we need to respond to him with our love: more than anything else it's our love he longs for.

Faith in Jesus

3rd Sunday of Advent (1980)

Happy is the man who does not lose faith in me.

David Pawson tells the story of an evangelist, Gordon Bailey, who was out parish-visiting during a mission. At one house the man opened the door and Gordon said:

'If you've got a moment I'd like to talk to you about Jesus.'
'I'm not interested in religion,' the man replied.
'Who mentioned anything about religion?'
'Well, you did.'
'No, I didn't,' countered Gordon.
'Well anyway,' said the man, 'you won't get me to church.'
'Who mentioned anything about church?'
'You did,' said the man, 'didn't you?'

There was a moment's silence, and then Gordon suggested the best thing to do was start the conversation all over again. So they shut the door, Gordon rang the bell, and the man opened the door a second time. And Gordon began again:

'If you have a moment to spare, I'd like to talk to you about Jesus.'
The man said, 'I'm still not interested.'
'What, not interested in the most famous man that ever lived?'
'Well, I wouldn't quite put it like that ...'
'What do you know about him?' asked Gordon. 'Do you know how he died?'
'Yes, he died on a cross. Crucified.'
'Correct. But do you know that thousands of other people were crucified in those days?'
'No. I'd never thought about it.'
'So don't you think it's a strange thing that out of all those people who were crucified, you've only heard of one?'

The man yielded and invited Gordon in and they talked about Jesus for more than those few minutes.

Several points stand out in this story. The main one is the truth that many people mix up Jesus with religion and church. They get them the wrong way round. Mention Jesus and immediately they rush in with 'I've no time for church, I'm not the religious sort. I worship God in my own way.' They've got hold of the wrong end of the stick and put the cart before the horse. It's not Jesus who wants us to go to Church, it's the Church who wants us to go to Jesus, wants to tell us about Jesus and why he was born and what he died for. And we, if we've got it round the right way, go to Church because the Church and her priests and ministers can teach us about Jesus, put us right where we have gone wrong.

This Advent season we are going through at present: is it on about religion, about Church? No, it's telling us all about the coming of our Saviour and how to get ready for him. We need to start the conversation again each year, because each year we may have taken a wrong turning and may be getting further and further away from the true Jesus and the truth Jesus came to teach us.

John the Baptist is an example of what I'm thinking. If you remember, Jesus' birth took place at a time of oppression. Israel was subject to the harsh Roman rule. And John the Baptist is a prisoner of conscience, deprived of his freedom for speaking out against the ruler. He must have asked the question we all ask today: where is this God of love? We see so little evidence of his reign, his kingdom, in our society, and feel far more conscious of tragedies, personal and national, like the death of John Lennon or an earthquake or tsunami. So John naturally sent messengers to Jesus: 'Are you the one who is to come or have we to wait for someone else?' And Jesus replied: 'Tell him, the blind see ... the deaf hear ... and happy is the man who does not lose faith in me' (Mt 11:4–6). Here we must understand that it is spiritual blindness and deafness that we are dealing with.

Millions prepare for and celebrate Christmas, but millions fail to see Jesus at its source, they're blind. Millions, like John the Baptist, in their prisons of one kind or another have to struggle to find meaning in their lives and answers to their questions, but they are deaf to the message of Jesus. Like 'our man at the door' many men and women fail to hear, fail to listen to what God is saying to them. If people cannot even hear properly what is said how will they ever listen with the ears of faith and hear God speaking to them through the words of scripture?

It is a matter of *faith* ultimately.

> He came to his own country and his own people did not receive him. Some, however, did receive him and believe in him and he gave them the right to be children of God (Jn 1:12).

Did you know that one of the chief signs of lack of faith is inattention. Raymond Nogar (in his book *Lord of the Absurd*) speaks of the 'Agnosticism of Inattention'. Our 'man at the door' was inattentive, he wasn't listening to what Gordon was saying. If you want to check on your own faith, check first on your attention. Do sermons pass you by? Do you neglect to attend to and answer the responses at Mass? Do you, deliberately, let your mind wander, daydream, switch on to another channel and try to distract yourself with trivialities? These are all forms of inattention and lack of faith.

But if we listen with faith, and try to be as attentive as humanly possible at Mass, we can, like John the Baptist even while still in his dungeon and about to be executed, believe that Jesus is the one who is to come and is even now among us – and 'Happy is the man who does not lose faith in (me) him.'

Ambiguous Advent

3rd Sunday of Advent (1983)

There are two sides to every coin, and for many people the experience of life itself is ambiguous. Is there anyone here, adult or child, male or female, old or young who does not feel the fluctuations of life? Up one minute, down the next; success one day, failure the next; too much to do one day, bored the next; times of sorrow followed by times of joy. At every party there will be one person who does not fit in, at every wedding there will be the unhappily married couple, or the lonely spinster. At every Mass there will be someone who is bored. And it is particularly at such seasons as Christmas, times of joy, that can sharpen the grief of those who suffer. It can rub in, as it were, the sorrow of those who have suffered a bereavement or divorce, or who have a dear one away or in hospital. The sense of emptiness seems worse. It can happen to children of poor families who see the expensive gifts of other children. 'Why can't we have a Christmas tree in our window like the others in the street?' – I heard that very question asked this week.

Although there are these special cases where the sorrow is particularly deep, I would venture to say that it is the same for all to some extent. There's always someone who seems to be better off, and if that doesn't spoil things, then there is the sorry state of the world with enough violence and terrorism, enough poverty and oppression to take the edge off most people's enjoyment of Christmas.

I think you'll agree this is a fairly good description of how Christmas comes over to most of us. Now this ambiguity, this mixture is something we may feel is wrong; it shouldn't be like that. And what you are expecting – even hoping – I'm going to tell you, is a nice simple solution, an easy remedy to apply which will help you to 'just forget your troubles and learn to say, "Christmas'll be a lovely day"'. Well, I'm going to have to disappoint you!

This is what Advent is all about. This sense of grappling with failure, with loss, with suffering; this search for a deeper joy beyond the trials of life is precisely what makes Advent such an important time for us all – something more than one mad rush to buy presents, send cards and make all the preparations for Christmas day. It's this very feeling of emptiness, this experience of the ambiguity of it all, that makes us long for the coming of the Holy One of God who alone can bring us true joy, who alone can wipe away every tear from our eyes. Moreover, it helps concentrate our minds – even if only for a few moments at a time – on the scripture texts.

The first readings are taken from the prophets, those great watchmen of the past. Isaiah is a special favourite, so full of comforting messages about the coming of God's anointed one. 'Have courage, fear not, behold your God.'

Then, St James, in the second reading today appeals to us to be patient: 'Do not lose heart because the Lord's coming will be soon.' Patience is a particularly important virtue during Advent which is a time of waiting. We live in a very impatient world where people seem incapable of postponing for a minute their needs and pleasures. It's what my mother called the 'must-have-now' syndrome. Children, the immature adolescent and the inadequate adult are poor at controlling their impulses. They must satisfy immediately any want, and can't bear a delay. If they are thwarted they sulk, throw temper-tantrums, get depressed. How sad it is to hear of children who have already had their Christmas presents. It shows how poor their parents are in impulse management. These children will go into marriage 'must-having' everything immediately. We all need to watch ourselves and guard against this 'must-have-now' syndrome. When St James urges us to be patient, to defer our needs, to exercise impulse control, he's bang up to date. Besides, to postpone one's own needs gives us a good opportunity to stop and think of others!

And the chief *other* we need to try and think about at this time is our Saviour, Jesus. And that is where the gospel of the day comes in with its questions about who Jesus is. Yes, we too have to keep asking these same old questions, for we too have to find and recognise Jesus when and where he comes to us today, in our present world.

And so then, be comforted if your lot this Christmas is not all that it might be. Try and put your disadvantage to advantage and grow in awareness of the deeper values of our faith.

Are you he who is to come

3rd Sunday of Advent (1998)

The message of John to Jesus is curious. He asks, 'Are you he who is to come, or have we to wait for another?' There's a telescoping of time. How can you be here now and still be coming in the future? There's something very Advent about it. In Advent there is this sense of already and not yet.

You have to remember that the Jews of Jesus' time were all expecting a Messiah. The prophets have been foretelling the coming of a great leader who would put everything right: jobs for everyone, minimum wage for the lower paid, social and health benefits for all, no more congestion on the roads. If that were to happen here in England, it would be equivalent to saying the time has come and now is when the sort of Messiah the Jews were expecting had come. That was the kind of man they were all expecting and John, who had his suspicions about Jesus, wanted to know if he was the man who was to come. According to the signs, it looked very much like it.

Here we are, 2,000 years later, and we find ourselves asking the same question about the Church. Are you the Church Christ founded or are we to look for another? Alas too many of our young people do go looking for another and end up in some sect or other. What makes them do this? Do they think the Church isn't delivering the goods? Is it that there isn't much of the evidence we would expect of a Church that Jesus founded?

There was a good answer to this given by one of the Catholic Evidence Guild who used to speak to the crowds at Hyde Park Corner – You don't hear of them these days. One of the hecklers from the crowd, a dirty and unkempt man, shouted out: 'Religion has been around for a long time and hasn't done much good, so what's the point?' The priest replied: 'Quite right, my man. But remember soap has been around for a very long time and it doesn't seem to have done you much good.' The great difficulty we are up against is not that the Church, still less Jesus Christ, has failed. It's not that it's been tried and found wanting. It's that it's been tried and found to be too difficult for many. People prefer their own comforts and selfish ways to the discipline of following Jesus – the Way, the Truth and the Life.

We have then, to take our question a stage further: we must ask the same question: 'Are you he who is to come, or must we look for another?' This time, however, we must put it in the mouths of those *outside* the Church, asking it of us *inside* the Church. Let me expand that question a bit more to see what they can legitimately expect of us. Is there any evidence in us of Jesus being for us the Way, the Truth and the Life? Or do we keep our light so hidden under a bushel that no one can see it or detect it? More to the point, is there any evidence that we have tried this 'soap' and that others so like the fragrance and the pleasant effect that they want to use it too? Someone made the good point: if we were dragged off before the magistrate for our faith, would there be enough evidence to convict us?

If John asked Jesus if he was the one who was to come, John also had messengers from the Pharisees who asked him who he was and, 'What answer shall we give those who sent us?' Today more than ever, people are looking to the Church for guidance, for answers to the questions our modern world keeps thrusting at us. That's the kind of answer we need to be giving those people. I was speaking with a Christian comedian recently and he was saying how hard it was to keep off the bad language and the smutty jokes that have become the stock-in-trade of comedians these days. He has held out on several occasions and got his way. But his career will not be so meteoric as a result. He gave a clear message to those who employ him of what the Christian values are. If only we could influence the ratings by not viewing certain programmes!

The question we have been considering so far today was: 'Are you the one who is to come or are we to await another?' Christ has certainly come, and the Church is his presence among us for all time. Yet, it is also true to say, he is still the one who is to come. He has come, but not yet wholly come. We live always in a kind of Advent, not just during this particular season before Christmas. We are always waiting for the Messiah to come, to come a little bit more as each of us grows a little bit more in the knowledge and love of Jesus. 'Be patient, brothers, until the Lord's coming' (Jas 5:7).

Jesus has been born according to the flesh in the stable at Bethlehem of Judea. He must now be born according to the Spirit in each of our souls. During the whole of our lives from Baptism to the grave Jesus is being born in us. It's never a once and for all. We must ever be transforming ourselves in Christ, taking on the dispositions of his heart, the judgements of his mind. That's the whole meaning and purpose of being a Christian, being transformed bit by bit into Christ until we become sons and daughters of the Father.

May Our Lady who nurtured the baby Jesus growing in her womb help us. May Jesus grow more and more and we grow less and less.

Pointing Sunday

4th Sunday of Advent (2004)

There is an old African story told about a group of Europeans who took a safari on the Serengeti. Their guide, Mousa, was an experienced and knowledgeable African. Anxious to see as many elephants, zebras, gazelles, lions and wildebeests, as possible, they pushed poor Mousa to the limit. Gulping rather than savouring each moment, they fell victim to the proverbial 'had-the-experience-missed-the-meaning' syndrome. Mousa called a halt, 'I can go no further, I'll have to wait for my spirit to catch up with me.' The equivalent of that in our own society is surely 'shop-till-you-drop' – I can go no further!

This last Sunday of Advent is a call to call a halt, and to wait for your spirit to catch up with you. The gospel account is factual: 'This is how Jesus Christ came to be born.' That's the reason for the season. It is pointing us to the drama that will soon enfold, and we need pointing. Why? Because in our world of image, television, voyeurism, of much loneliness and suffering, we desperately need to be directed towards healing and transformation. The Feast of the great Presence, of Emmanuel is approaching.

All through Advent there has been much pointing; we have been told to look – not at television, at glossy magazines, at the papers, but – to *look at things*: at mountains and valleys, at deserts and dry land, at wolves and lambs, lions and oxen. It has been *pointing at people*, particularly at John the Baptist: pointing at his clothing and his food, at what he was doing (baptising) and what he was saying (repent). It was asking people what they were going out into the desert to see: a reed? Fine clothes? Palaces? No, to see a prophet. The passage ends with 'Look, I am going to send my messenger before you; he will prepare the way of the Lord'. Finally we were told: 'Here is your God'; 'Look, your God is coming'.

In the second reading the Church gives us a passage from Romans to look at. Most of Paul's letters were written to churches he had founded, but Romans is an exception. It was written to a church founded by others to prepare the way for a later visit by Paul. His opening sentences are to reassure his hearers that the gospel he offers them is consistent with that preached by the other apostles; it's all about the Good News of what God has done for us in his Son, Jesus Christ: 'This news is about the Son of God, who according to the human nature he took was a descendant of David ... who in the order of the spirit ... was proclaimed Son of God in all his power.' The passage makes a perfect reading for this last Sunday of Advent. It's exactly what we are about to celebrate at Christmas.

The reason for the season of Christmas is the birth of Jesus. Who is this child? Isaiah says: 'A maiden is with child ... whom she will call Emmanuel, a name which means God-with-us' (Isa 7:14). In the gospel, we have Matthew's approach to the nativity quite different to Luke's account of the Annunciation. Matthew's annunciation is to Joseph. He says, straightforwardly enough:

> Do not be afraid to take Mary home as your wife, because she has conceived what is in her by the Holy Spirit. She will give birth to a son and you must name him Jesus, because he is the one who will save his people from their sins (Mt 1:18–25).

The reason for the season. If the two accounts differ, it's only in their approach. They are both affirming their faith in the origins of Jesus, even as St Paul does in Romans. Jesus is not simply the product of human evolution, but the definitive intervention of God in human history. 'See I am doing a new thing.' What St John of the Cross calls 'the all of God'.

Taken together, the three readings show the two perspectives on the life of Jesus. On the one hand, he is a product of human history, born of a woman, descended from David. On the other, he is Emmanuel, God-with-us, the Son of God, conceived by the Holy Spirit. It is this mystery of Christ's two natures, human and divine, which we are about to ponder once more in our celebration of Christmas.

The two middle Sundays of Advent concentrated on John the Baptist, today our attention is directed to Mary and Joseph and the child: 'Emmanuel' – God-with-us. Think back to those travellers in the

Serengeti anxious to see everything and miss nothing. It needed Mousa to call a halt and let his spirit catch up with him to show them what they were missing. The readings today are making sure we miss nothing. A Nigerian proverb says, 'Listen, and you will hear the footsteps of the ants.' Today we are challenged to listen and hear the footsteps of God who is coming into our lives in ordinary ways, through ordinary people and at ordinary moments of our lives. If the name of the son to be born is called Emmanuel – God-with-us – to what extent is 'God-with-us'? To what extent do people look upon us and recognise the presence of the Lord in us and in our Church?

Reality Revealed (Transfiguration)

2nd Sunday of Lent (1987)

If this (the story of the Transfiguration we have just read) is the other side of Jesus, which is the real one: the transfigured, dazzling and glorious one, the beloved Son, hobnobbing with the great men of old? Or, the 'Jesus only', the figure on the crucifix, jeered at and spat upon? I put it this way because we experience a similar problem in our own lives: which is the real me? Where do I really become fully alive: in the home, at work, at Mass? Everyone wants to be where the action is: but where is the action for you or for me? At one time we may think it is to be a star performer, sportsman or pop-idol; the next moment we think maybe we ought to be in the boardroom where all the decisions are taken. Peter must've felt a bit like that when he exclaimed: 'It is good to be here. Let us build three tents.' He really felt they had arrived, this was it. It was, for a few glorious moments, but then within minutes the apparition had faded and there was 'only Jesus'. Worse than that, there was all this talk of the coming Passion, as if *that* was where the real action was to take place, not here on Mt Tabor.

You may understand more exactly what I'm getting at if you think about that curious phrase we have: 'Out there, there's the real world.' The surprising part about this phrase is that it's not just you or I who use it, everyone else is using it – soldiers, doctors, bankers, teachers, parents, priests. 'My boy, my girl, just wait till you go into the real world!' How often have people told me I'm wasting my life here: 'Get out into the real world, you could do so much good there.' What is the real world? Where is the action? Aren't we real enough here this morning? Though even the priest would seem to imply something of the sort, for when he dismisses the congregation he says, 'Go in peace, to love and serve the Lord', as if you weren't really loving and serving the Lord at Mass – and more so here than at any other time or place in your lives.

That complaint you sometimes hear: 'I don't go to Mass anymore, it all seems so irrelevant' has this type of experience in mind. But I'm sure most of us, precisely because our ordinary, everyday lives seem so empty of meaning, so untransfigured, come gladly to Mass to get a glimpse of Jesus and a breath of some supernatural air. We come to Mass because it is our central act of worship. The folk hymn expresses this when it says: The reason I live is to worship you. The very reason of creation is to give my life back to God in worship. It's the reason why I'm here. If that's not the heart that beats at the very centre of our heart then our lives are empty. That was why the Transfiguration was such a wonderful moment. They saw what they were worshipping, they came close to the divinity of Jesus.

However, such moments can't last in this vale of tears. And St Peter in one of his letters must have been thinking about this when he wrote:

> You love him although you have not seen him, and you believe him although you do not now see him. So you rejoice with a great joy which words cannot express, because you are receiving the salvation of your souls which is the purpose of your faith.

A bit further on he continues: 'So then, have your minds ready for action' (1 Pet 1:8–9). Keep alert and set your hope completely on the blessing which will be given you when Jesus Christ is revealed.' The word revealed suggests he was thinking of what he had seen when Jesus was Transfigured. Notice how the whole structure of the passage is based on the three theological virtues: faith, hope and love. You *love* him though you haven't seen him. You *believe* in him though you don't see him now. Finally, you hope in the future blessings when Jesus will be revealed and we shall *see* him as he is. In other words, even though we can't *see* the Transfigured Jesus now, we go on as if we had, for *if* we *had* seen him, we couldn't love him or believe in him or hope in him in quite the same way.

It would seem, therefore, that there are some grounds for us to think of the real world as some imaginary *out there*, a Transfiguration spot where all is transparent and significant. Whilst what we are actually living and experiencing, real enough though it is, always seems or appears to be unimportant and ordinary. I can well believe members of the Royal Family sometimes wish they could be like normal people 'out there', and walk about the town without any fuss or security. Again I remember reading during the Falkland's conflict about one soldier who complained: 'This isn't what I joined for.' I ask you, what is a soldier's job: marching up and down on the parade ground? In the navy, they have a saying: 'You joined!' That means to say: What did you join for if you are complaining about what you've got? Did you expect life in the navy to be all leave in port?

The Church, then, wisely reminds us of what the real business of Lent is really about: not some 'out there' place, not sitting above the clouds on Mt Tabor, but getting to grips with reality: the reality of my sinfulness, my need of salvation, for faith, hope and love. The reality of the people I live with. As St Peter said: 'So, then, have your minds ready for action. Keep alert and set your hope completely on the blessing which will be given you when Jesus Christ is revealed.'

If you only knew the Gift of God

3rd Sunday of Lent (1987)

There were two quotes that caught my attention in the gospel: 'If you knew what God is offering' or, in another translation: 'If you only knew the Gift of God.' The other text was: 'He has told me all I have ever done.'

'If you only knew the Gift of God.' I can remember the impact this text had on me years ago. All God had done for me and what was I doing for him? Jesus is almost saying: 'If you *did* know, you'd be at a loss.' As it is we don't. The Bible even tells us as much: 'The eye has not seen, nor ear heard, nor has it entered into the heart of man what things God has prepared for those who love him' (1 Cor 2:9). We sometimes get glimpses of what God has done for us in the beauty of nature, the goodness of people, the sheer exhilaration of being alive. But these are things. Jesus doesn't mean things here, he means *himself*. He's the Gift of God. Again, we occasionally get a glimpse of what Jesus means to us in our lives. His forgiveness, his grace, his love, his Words to us in the Scriptures. But do any of us ever fully grasp 'what a friend I have in Jesus'?

When speaking of *gifts* in human terms, most people automatically think in terms of presents, a thing; and the more expensive the more we prize it. In Scripture, however, the Gift of God has a particular meaning. It is found in the Come, Holy Ghost, 'the Gift of God's right hand' (*the Donum Dei of the Veni Creator Spiritus*). It means the gift of God's love, and God's love comes to us through the person of the Holy Spirit dwelling within us. St Paul is directing our attention to this (in the second reading): 'This hope is not deceptive, because the *love of God* has been *poured* (not trickled) into our hearts by the Holy Spirit which has been given us' (Rom 5:4–5). Is this what Jesus means when he says, 'if you only knew the Gift of God'? If we only knew what it means to have his love, his Holy Spirit dwelling in us, what a transformation it would bring about in our lives and thinking. Not only that, but it would enable us to get a glimpse of God himself. 'God is love', St John tells us. We must go even further and say, it would show us the constancy of God's purpose, what he is doing in us through his Spirit, bringing us into the image of his Son, so that 'we are not only called children of God, but *are*'. This is the Gift of God – what God is offering.

During the week I was introduced to the writings of Nicholas von Zindendorf. Nicholas was born in Germany in 1700 and grew up to be a great protestant missionary. He records, as an adult, how even at four years of age he made his first commitment: 'In my fourth year I began to seek God earnestly and determined to become a servant of Jesus Christ.' When he was nineteen he saw the famous picture by Sternberg, known as 'Behold the Man'. It shows Jesus being led out by Pilate. The caption underneath is: 'All this I have done for you. What have you done for me?' Nicholas acknowledged how much he had received through his family, his education and his wealth, but went on to ask:

> Although I have sought to serve Jesus I feel I have really done so very little for him. I look at that picture of him and realise that he has paid the supreme price for me, but I wonder what on earth I have done for him in return?

Nicholas was able to itemise what God had done for him in this world's goods. But it was this picture that was to inspire his whole life, for it brought home to him something of this gift of God: what God had done for him, what God was doing for him, and what God was going to do for him in the future – in spiritual terms. St Paul was urged on by similar sentiments: 'The love of God urges us.' And today we heard him tell us:

> It is not easy to die for a good man – though of course for someone really worthy, a man might be prepared to die – but what proves that God loves us is that Christ died for us while we were still sinners.

If we could only grasp a fraction of what God is doing and offering us.

The reason why I mentioned the other text was because it brings out the paradox: 'He has told me all that I have ever done.' This is the worrying thing. She meant all the bad things, not all the good things.

'All this I have done for you, what have you done for me?' Weighed in the scales: all the things I shouldn't have done outweigh the things I should have done. Like the scene of the woman taken in adultery, where Our Lord says: 'Let him who is without sin cast the first stone,' they all began to leave, starting with the eldest. As the prophet Isaiah says: 'What more could I have done for my vineyard? Why did it yield wild grapes in return for all my care?' There is only one answer to this paradox and St Therese puts it this way:

> Happy indeed am I to die and go to heaven, but when I think of those words of our Lord: 'Behold, I come quickly, and my reward is with me to render to every man according to his own works.' (Rev 22:12) I reflect that he will be very much embarrassed as regards me: I have no works … Well, he will render to me according to his own works.

Without a doubt, the first and most important thing we must do with regard to this Gift of God is to receive it and acknowledge it with love and gratitude. And, then, and only then, set about trying to make some small return for this Gift. Let the water, welling up within us, overflow to others in kindness and forgiveness, thoughtfulness and encouragement.

Freedom of choice –
Sin – both Action & State

3rd Sunday of Lent (1969)

In Genesis, Adam had to make a choice between God and the forbidden fruit. We too have to make the same choice. Since the success or failure of our lives depends on our freedom of choice and the choices we make, it is worth devoting a little time to think about it.

Something we must never forget is that sin is not to choose something that is bad, but to choose something that seems to offer us a good, as when a man steals £10. He sees the value of that money and wants it. But it is a selfish good for he has not considered that, from the point of view of the person from whom he steals it, the loss is a definite evil.

Stealing is not the only sin, but the point I want to make clear is that life is made up of many choices between the various goods of this earth. This may sound obvious, yet from it follow two very significant aspects about life which it is easy to overlook. First, as long as we are here on earth we can never make a once and for all choice between God and finite goods. One often thinks it would be very nice to make a final decision – get it over and done with like having a tooth out. It would save us a lot of trouble if we did not have to worry anymore about being able to make a mistake. But we can't enjoy the type of freedom God has given us unless we retain this power of choice. The angels had to make a 'once and for all' decision for or against God; they had one choice, one chance. We have lots of choices and so lots of chances. It is a mixed blessing. All is not lost if we make the wrong choice, provided, however, we don't make the same wrong choice again.

The other thing about life, freedom of choice explains, is the feeling we have of never being absolute masters of ourselves; we never possess our life – be it married life or religious life or even our salvation – entirely at any one moment. This wouldn't matter if only we could be sure our goodwill would last. But, since the Fall, our lasting goodwill and that of others is not guaranteed to last. We know this all too well from the fact that people do get divorced and priests do go off the rails even though they started off with the best of intentions.

An example of these two points will help make them clearer. If you get married, in one sense it is a final decision – a once and for all. In another sense, it has got to be renewed in actual practice every day. Each day, that initial decision has got to be worked out afresh in the choices one makes between the various goods – goods for one's self, one's partner and one's children. And because of our weak wills, there will always remain a certain amount of uneasiness even in the best of marriages.

Whilst this freedom of choice lasts, sin remains possible. That means to say, 'we are daily in danger' as St Paul warns us 'of incurring God's anger and ceasing to be children of light'. However, from the fact that no choice is final, no sin irrevocable, we not unreasonably conclude, 'ah, plenty more chances', 'it isn't a final decision', 'it is over and done with and so doesn't really matter provided I don't do the same thing next time'. No, it does matter for the very important reason that sin is not only an action, sin is also a state. Often our attitude to sin is that of the driver with his eye on the mirror keeping a watch out for a police car behind. Provided he doesn't get caught, he thinks, no harm can come if he breaks the speed limit. Sin is an action of this kind, but it is also something more. Sin affects the person who does it, it *makes* him a certain kind of person. A man, for instance, who commits a murder, commits it and it is done, yes. But what has happened to this man who deprived another of his life? He has become a murderer. You can see my point surely? His whole personality has been involved, he has become identified with his crime. The same thing happens if you have your driving licence endorsed. Even though the offence is over and done with, you are now a certain kind of a driver – a driver who drives without due care and attention.

Things we do by mistake, like breaking a window, are harmless in that we remain personally unaffected. But we can't tell a lie or be dishonest without becoming a liar or a thief. It is very easy to miss this step out. One can say in confession, 'I've told three lies' but we fail to realise that this means I'm a liar. And the more often we repeat such acts the more deeply identified we become with that type of person. Confession can obtain pardon for the offence to God, but it does not wipe out the scars they leave on our character.

As I said, no decision we make is a once and for all one and hence we can never possess our life entirely at any one moment. Nevertheless each decision is somehow affecting our whole life. We are creatures of habit and what may have been originally a deliberate choice very soon becomes an unthinking habit which we cannot help or perhaps don't even notice. You can see why St Paul is always on about sin and virtue. These determine the type of person we are: saints or sinners. And so, even though it is consoling to know all is not lost no matter how bad we are, at the same time let us learn from the Gospel that a house swept and garnished won't remain that way long without constant and repeated effort.

I've said these few things today because, from time to time, it is a good thing to remind ourselves about the nature of our human choice. Monotonous, everyday life with its seemingly trivial details, can blind us to the great risks involved in our every action, our every decision.

The awakening of the woman of Samaria

3rd Sunday of Lent (1996)

Today's dialogue between Jesus and the Samaritan woman (Jn 4:1–42) is a revelation in itself. It would need a whole course of lectures to fill out all the hidden themes contained in it.

Where this passage is so striking is that it only happened because the woman was prepared; she was ready to face her own shortcomings; the water she drank daily had got stale and no longer refreshed her, her love life was in tatters. She was tired too of the daily toil to come and draw water. The prospect of getting water that she didn't have to fetch was very attractive.

The first point that Jesus makes her realise are the things she takes for granted. If only you knew what God is offering and who it is that is saying to you: 'Give me a drink.' We think we know Jesus. We even take him for granted. In some respects this 'taking things for granted' is the vice of our age. People take it for granted that Jesus will be there whenever they should need him, that the churches will always be there, that priests and religious will always be there to marry them, baptise and teach their children, bury their dead, so they don't bother to attend church regularly or do anything to deepen their faith.

Yet, paradoxically, the woman makes a profound reply: 'The well is deep: how could you get this living water?' We live in an age of two types of culture: the deep cultures which are hard to acquire and the shallow cultures which most people paddle in because they don't have to learn to swim and are so shallow there is no danger of their getting out of their depths. The deep culture (of which our religion is a kind) requires you devote time and thought and energy to acquire. The shallow culture is absorbed through the media. What is such a shame is how unaware people are of this. What is more serious is how easily and noiselessly the quick-fit culture wreaks havoc on the other, more difficult and deep cultures. Young people leave family and home, they leave churches, they even leave the institution of marriage for the

37

seemingly easier one of cohabitation. The well *is* deep: and to achieve anything of real depth and lasting value is a long pull.

It is probably true that most of us, most of the time, are only marginally in touch with the full range of what is going on around us and within us. Acquiring culture is the least of our worries, or at least it would be except for the fact that we are breathing in the shallow culture all the time. Most of our waking hours are spent carrying out daily tasks: like the woman toiling to fetch water each day, or the apostles who have gone off to find food; travelling to and from one village to the next. We spend most of our time on 'autopilot'. But, given the right circumstances, we do 'de-automatise'. We wake up and become very conscious of the here and now. You can do this by consciously taking thought for where you are now – in church, in God's presence, assisting at Mass, and asking yourself what am I doing here? Quite often, though, we are pulled out of our dreamworld into the present by something beautiful, or a surprise, or a sudden shock, or a personal disaster. Instead of being driven along by circumstances and by habit, we wake up and become aware and start asking questions.

This is evidently what happened when the woman met Jesus. The whole dialogue is punctuated with questions which reveal her desire to find answers to problems she'd been living with, or, should I say, to find deeper answers than the ones she'd been taking for granted – on autopilot. She is looking for more than the shallow culture has to offer.

A little illustration comes to mind. Every so often a chaffinch hops onto the ledge outside my window and appears to be looking in. I don't know what attracts it there since there is no food, but it still comes back. I look at him and wonder if he looks at me. I think: 'Is he just seeing himself reflected in the glass, or is he seeing through the glass into the room?' Is he seeing me, or worse, is he seeing through me? Or better, is he seeing not me but Jesus dwelling in me? This is an example of what happens to people like the Samaritan woman? Instead of just seeing herself in the glass, reflecting the shallow culture of the world, she begins to see through it, just as she begins to see Jesus is more than just a Jew: 'Come and see a man who has told me everything I ever did; I wonder if he is the Christ?' She begins to want the whole truth, to ask what lies beyond, not just what the world tells her is true. 'You worship what you do not know,' Jesus told her. 'The hour will come when true worshippers will worship the Father in spirit and truth.'

Each of us here today is meeting Jesus in this gospel reading, each of us is reaching down into the well, into the depth of Christ's mystery. Each of us wants to see through the sham, the false, the pretence in our lives, and to do that we must be open to what he is asking, no matter what the consequence, no matter where it leads. You may not know where it will lead, you just have to be ready to follow; to be open – wide open! Mind you, being open does not mean being gullible. It may mean challenging what is being said. The woman certainly challenged Jesus. But she challenged from an attitude of openness, not of stubbornness. The woman was ready to learn, or should I say unlearn, for that is what openness means.

So, in the clear and deep waters of the well the eternal truths are reflected: aspects of the faith we may have been taking for granted because we lived on autopilot. The well is deep. Let us turn to Jesus and ask him to help us draw water from this wellspring of life-giving water.

Jacob's Well

3rd Sunday of Lent (1999)

The Samaritan woman could easily take place in the twentieth century. She was, like so many, very unsatisfied with her lot. She had drunk at several wells and still not found what she was looking for. Today's Samaritan is likely to drink at many wells too: wells of power, of learning, of success, of money, of travel and of pleasure, and still not find any deep sense of contentment, still not be at ease. Material things cannot and never will satisfy the thirsting of the human spirit. God has created a hunger and a thirst in us that only he can satisfy.

The tragedy of our times is that so many people are looking in the wrong places for the answers to the unresolved problems of this life. The human condition is short on two things: knowledge and power. For all the information technology, we are no nearer to finding the sort of knowledge we want, namely, the answers to life's questions and to the breakdown of the moral structures and institutions that have held society together for so long. The trouble is God doesn't speak through the internet or through the media. We won't find him there. They are filling our minds with all sorts of mostly irrelevant information. God speaks to us through his word and teachings, through our own searching and praying. It's not more extraterrestrial space exploration we need but more inner space exploration. It's in that inner space that we will discover God. 'The hour is coming when true worshippers will worship the Father in spirit and in truth' (Jn 4:23). There we will find that God is with us through his power and presence. There will be less chance of our putting God to the test as the Israelites did, by saying, 'Is the Lord with us, or not?'

Not finding the knowledge and power in wealth or on the internet, things that are for the most part elusive and illusory, many, sadly, turn to the occult. The word 'occult' means 'hidden', or 'secret'. Whenever people seek either knowledge or power from any hidden or secret source other than God, then they are opening themselves up to the realm of evil spirits.

Some people seek knowledge and are often hooked by curiosity. The Ouija board, for instance, spells out answers to our questions about our future, or about the fate of dead loved ones. Parents may want to know if their son who committed suicide is happy in the afterlife – a very human question. A seemingly harmless desire, but in seeking forbidden (should we call it 'sensitive'?) knowledge, they open themselves to demonic influences. Astrology and fortune telling are more benign ways of trying to obtain knowledge, especially foreknowledge, but it remains knowledge God does not intend us to have.

The same is true of people who seek power. Practitioners of black magic, witch doctors, sects and the like are there for those who seek to influence people and events by occult practices. It is through these two desires for knowledge and power that people become more and more involved with witchcraft and satanism.

Why this is relevant to today's story is that the key to this dialogue between Jesus and the Samaritan is knowledge and power. The woman said to Jesus, 'I know that the Messiah – that is, Christ – is coming; and when he comes he will tell us everything.' 'I am speaking to you,' said Jesus, 'I am he.' Jesus had already explained to her, 'You worship what you do not know, we worship what we do know.' The woman goes back to the village and tells everyone, 'Come and see a man who has told me everything I ever did; I wonder if he is the Christ?' To know Jesus and he who sent him is all we need to know. As we had in the Laud's antiphon: 'Chosen and called in the one body, may we know the love of God which is beyond all knowledge' (Col 3:15). It's true there is much we do not understand and many things we would dearly love to know, but 'my grace is sufficient for you'.

The woman found the knowledge she needed, and she was also offered the power of living water:

> Whoever drinks this water will get thirsty again; but anyone who drinks the water that I shall give will never be thirsty again: the water that I shall give will turn into a spring inside him, welling up to eternal life (Jn 4:14).

Of course the woman eagerly asked for that kind of water, as anyone would and we do. This power, the true power, the power of the Holy Spirit has been poured into our hearts. St Paul understood this power so well: 'Jesus told him: "My grace is all you need, for my power is strongest when you are weakest." I am most happy to be proud of my weaknesses, in order to feel the protection of Christ's power over me.' (2 Cor 12:9–10).

This sets the scene. In the final analysis, we are called to union with God in Christ. This is the 'Gift of God' which Jesus only wished we knew. By grace we can share in it and grow in knowledge of God and union with him. St Paul, writing to the Philippians, puts it thus:

> I am confident of this, that the one who has begun a good work among you will bring it to completion by the day of Christ Jesus ... for all of you share in God's grace with me ... and this is my prayer, that your Love may overflow more and more with knowledge and full insight ... (1:6, 7, 9).

Obviously, that doesn't all happen at once. The real power of the Spirit lies in the grace to wait for an understanding of what is happening through the events of our lives, knowing God's grace is sufficient for us. He never gives us more than we need but he will always give us enough to sustain and support us throughout our lives as we wait for the coming of our Saviour.

How free are we? The freer, the easier

Laetare Sunday (1969)

So then brethren, we are not children of the bond woman, but of the free; by the freedom wherewith Christ has made us free.

How free are we? You sometimes hear it argued that because we are able to sin we are freer than the angels who cannot. That is how a permissive society thinks and there is obviously some fault in the reasoning somewhere. Angels who are superior beings to men must be freer than we are. How is it, then, that they cannot sin? Sin is not a freedom but a slavery. Whenever men sin, it is not because they are more free but because they are less free. If a man murders, or steals, or takes his revenge, he does so because of all sorts of factors that have impaired the freedom of his judgement. Things like passion, lust, ignorance, hatred and envy. Surely one cannot say these make him more free? Is the man who is drunk and in a rage more free or less free than the man who is sober and in control of himself? That is why the angels are freer than we: they are free from all these factors that deceive and mislead us into choosing an evil course of action.

This applies in all spheres of life; we find it in the skills required at work or in some sport. Take a game like tennis. How does a man or woman become a Wimbledon champion? By making fewer mistakes than anyone else. And certainly, if you compare his/her game with that of the person at the local club, there can be no doubt as to whose is the freer and easier style. Yet, if we argue along the lines just mentioned, we would have to conclude that the person at the local club was freer because he/she makes more mistakes. The Wimbledon champion is less free because he/she can't so easily make a muck of a shot or a service.

In order to see fully the faultiness of our ideas on this question of freedom you have only to consider how we regard the performance of virtue. How often do we feel or think that the virtue that comes easily and naturally to us is less pleasing to God than the one we find hard and difficult to practise. For example, if a husband and wife find it easy to love one another and are tremendously fond of their children, we should conclude, according to this theory, that they love each other less than the husband and wife who have great difficulty. Why? Well, because it is easy for one and hard for the other.

Normally, the amount of difficulty we experience in performing a virtue means we are less good at it. So with the husband and wife: the greater their love, the easier it is for them to make the sacrifices. That does not mean to say these sacrifices will cost less, but it does mean we should not argue along the lines that there is more love in an unhappy marriage because it is harder. I agree, there may be more love on one side, just as our Lord had to love us a lot more because we love him so little in return.

We can see the same type of thing in a talented person and a non-talented one. The way a good pianist gets around the notes of a difficult piece leaves us spellbound. But, notice, how, although the difficulties require more skill and more practice, the fact remains it looks so terribly easy because his skill is master of it. Whereas for the musician with less talent such pieces are too difficult. Yet, we would certainly never say that because he finds them hard he has more talent than the musician who finds them easy.

There are three conclusions I would like to draw from these few points I have been making. First, to be able to sin is not freedom but the *want* of freedom. Doubts and passions and all the other things that lead us into sin are not liberating factors but enslaving ones. Sin is a slavery, as St Paul so often says. Consequently, we must avoid the fatal mistake of thinking that our freedom will suffer if we don't choose the wrong thing from time to time just to show I'm still free. God forbid. 'I won't go to Mass this week to show I'm still going freely.' What we should be saying is 'I will go to Mass this week to prove that I'm still free from all those obstacles which could prevent my going.'

Secondly, don't feel that because you love someone and find it easy to get on with them, or because you find it easy to be patient, good, kind and pure, that this is because you have less virtue than the person who finds it hard. It's doing the right thing that counts; whether it is easy or difficult is only secondary. After all, I sincerely hope that in heaven, being good will be the easiest and most natural thing.

The third point concerns how we might react according to whether we have talents or not. Ultimately, what we have comes from God. If he loves one person in such a way as to give him great talents and make certain things come easily, like the tennis champion or the great pianist, then that person must be ever at pains to realise it is a gift from God for which he must be grateful and for which he will have to give an account.

What about the person who has few gifts and many sins because God did not give him the graces to avoid them. This does not mean that God loves him less. The more sinful a person is the more love it demands on the part of God to forgive. God loves to forgive and in order to have people he could pour out his forgiveness on he did not give them all the gifts *they* needed so that they might need Him more. A man with great gifts tends to need God less. But the man with *few* tends to need God's merciful love more. God's love is a great mystery and why he loves some in this way and others in that is something 'God alone knows'.

The freedom Christ won for us and freedom St Paul is talking about in the epistle is this: To be able to sin is not freedom at all – certainly not in the way our permissive society thinks. Sin is a slavery as anyone who gets in its grip soon knows. 'So then, brethren, we are not children of the bond woman, but of the free, by the freedom wherewith Christ has made us free.'

The Christian's Death

5th Sunday of Lent (1984)

'If you had been here, my brother would not have died.' 'He opened the eyes of the blind man, could he not have prevented this man's death?' (Jn 11:21; 37)

With words like these we are drawn on another step in our Lenten pilgrimage. In last week's readings we were invited to see our blindness in the affairs of this life. This week we are confronted with our inability to see beyond the grave.

Many of the Jews still had no belief in the afterlife. The grave was the end. But some were already moving in that direction. Such prophecies as we heard in the first reading about 'dem dry bones gonna walk around' hinted as much. Martha and Mary certainly had faith in an afterlife: 'I know he will rise again at the resurrection on the last day.' Then Jesus came out with those unforgettable words: 'I am the resurrection. If anyone believes in me, even though he dies he will live, and whoever lives and believes in me will never die' (Jn 11:25–26).

How does he mean 'will never die'? Presumably, that means that death as we understand it is not really an end to life; we still live but no longer with our body and soul together. At death they become separated: the soul lives on and the body is consigned to the grave, where the matter rests until the last day when we will receive new, immortal bodies that can never die.

Last Sunday was Mother's Day and it's one thing we all have in common, we each have a mother. Without her we simply wouldn't be here; we wouldn't even be. The extraordinary thing is, it's almost impossible to think of ourselves as ever having not been. By the same token, we find it equally difficult to grasp the nettle of our own death. You're going to die and I'm going to die. You may live to a ripe old age or you may be like the young man of seventeen who got leukaemia and died aged twenty. His struggle lasted for three years and at times it looked as if he might make it. Towards the end, he admitted to his

46

mother and father how bad the pain in his hip was and then added: 'There, you have my complaints for the day, but it doesn't matter because I know I'm doing God's will.' His mother said to him, 'You realise, you know, you might die at any time, don't you?' 'Yes, of course,' he said, 'I've known that for years.' You don't have to be gone ninety before you understand those two fundamental principles: God's will as all-important, and the certainty of my death. How many young people here – and not so young – could have answered like that?

Death is a very mysterious thing – well, life is too. In our bleaker moments we long for it. Like St Paul we cry out, 'I long to have done and to be with Christ.' And then, like him we are forced to add: 'To die is gain but to live is Christ.' It is related of St Martin of Tours. When he was near to dying his brethren pleaded with him not to leave them. So he prayed: 'Lord, if I be necessary for them I will not refuse the toil.' He would have preferred the repose of death but was prepared to work on in the Lord's vineyard if that was the Lord's wish.

Although, in our impatience, we may long to be moving on to the next stage the fact is few of us are as ready to part with life as we think. This comes out most obviously when a person is dying, say of cancer. You can be sure when your turn comes the medical men will be the last people to tell you. Even the family are afraid to come clean. Everyone is afraid it may upset you, it may make you give up wanting to get better. We don't want that, nevertheless we do want to know when the chips are down. Dying is a difficult emotion to cope with. It's difficult for the person dying, and it's just as difficult for the family. Maybe that's why telling someone is so difficult. It's as hard to lose someone as it is for that someone to die. Often we tell people not to cry in order to spare ourselves the necessity of having to cope with tears. Not so Jesus. When all the others were crying over Lazarus' death he wept too.

'If you had been here,' both the sisters said to Jesus. He wasn't there and that is what made it so crushing for them. Then he arrives and Martha says to Mary: 'The Master is here and wants to see you.' And so it is with us, in our life and in our death. Jesus is present. With him present our natural grief and sorrow are contained within a spirit of hope and reassurance. Jesus not only weeps with us. He dies with us. He is there waiting for us. Death will not be the end for Jesus came to take away sin and death and to lead us to his Father.

In the light of Christ

5th Sunday of Lent (2002)

Today's gospel (raising of Lazarus) is one we are likely to hear when we attend a funeral. It's not just an affirmation of life, but also an affirmation of life beyond the earthbound life we know. The Lord tells Martha that he cannot only restore her brother to life in this world, he can raise him and anyone who believes in him to heavenly life in the next world.

During the week, a lady came into the shop, with more than her shopping list on her mind. It transpired that she had a tumour on the brain and it was inoperable. She asked me for a blessing. I blessed her and we prayed together. As we talked, I could tell how perplexed she was about why it should happen to her (she was in her late forties), how would she cope; her partner and friends were tending to desert her.

She was a churchgoer, but somehow she was one of those who 'read' this thing called life without making any sense of it; unlike other followers of Jesus who 'read' Jesus into the events of their life, and are thus able to make sense of it. Well, perhaps, if not make sense of it, at least bring their faith and trust into it. Someone once described life as 'a jigsaw puzzle with most of the pieces missing'. I would suggest it is better to say, life is a puzzle not with the pieces missing, but with the picture of what it's a puzzle of missing. If you try to piece the puzzle of life together without the picture of Jesus' life and death to guide you, you won't have a clue where all the bits go. All the bits of the puzzle are there, but they might as well be upside down if you don't have Jesus in front of you to follow and see where each bit fits in. In the story of the raising of Lazarus, Mary said, 'If you had been here, Lord, my brother would not have died.' Jesus then said, 'a man can walk in daytime without stumbling because he has the light to see by, but if he walks at night he stumbles because there is no light to see by (the picture).'

We Christians are no different than anyone else in the world. It's just as much a puzzle to us as it is to them. We come up against the same challenges and questions just as they do. We muddle and struggle along as best we can, just like they do. But our life in the light of Christ shows us a different way of looking at them and experiencing them. We have the completed picture to follow.

And the completed picture is, when a Christian comes to the end of his life, his life is changed not ended. Today's gospel has the astounding news: 'I am the resurrection and the life. Whoever believes in me, though he should die, will come to life; and whoever is alive and believes in me will never die' (Jn 11:25–26). Do you believe this? Do I believe this? Really believe, deep down, with all my mind and heart? Or am I hesitant and unsure? Can you say with Martha, 'Yea, Lord, I do believe: I really do believe my brother will rise again at the resurrection on the last day'? Then, you will stop gloomily looking down at your boot laces, worrying and wondering about how it will all end. Chesterton said, we should have our heads in the air, not our noses.

The lady with the tumour was still coming to terms with her condition. It is easy for us to be objective and philosophical about someone else's plight, but it's not as easy if it's your own. Nevertheless, I'd say one of the most pervasive evils of our day is wishful thinking – or what the experts call *denial*. It creeps into every aspect of life. But it is at its most poignant with someone who is terminally ill; neither the person him/herself, nor the family and friends want to admit it. *Denial* is what everyone feels is the positive way to approach it. But it's not. Jesus never denied his coming death. Recall the occasions when he foretold the Son of Man was going up to Jerusalem to be condemned to death. And what did St Peter do? Deny it! He told Jesus to put such thoughts behind him. And how Jesus rounded on him for trying to do so! It's an extraordinary characteristic of Jesus how he never denied. Notice how often he asserts who he is: 'I am the bread of life'; 'I am the resurrection and the life. If anyone believes in me, even though he dies he will live.' As we know, it was because he never denied and refused to deny who he was that caused him to be put to death.

It seems a good thought to put before you as we approach Our Lord's death. It's a vital question to tackle yourself with. What are the things in my life that I am in denial about? My faith is one (denying Jesus). My own death is another, or that of a close relative. Another obvious instance is some secret sin and need for confession. The psalmist was very conscious of his time on earth being limited: 'Lord make me know the shortness of life, that I may learn wisdom of heart.' That's the sort of wisdom that will help solve the jigsaw of life and death.

Emmaus Visited

3ʳᵈ Sunday after Easter (2002)

What are the Evangelists really trying to tell us about the Resurrection? That Jesus rose from the dead, surely? That his body was a risen body; there were no bones left in the tomb? Yes. They also emphasise that the apostles were to be witnesses. That's fairly clear. Yet whilst all that is true, there are a lot of ambiguities. It's never clear where he is, or is meant to be. The angel at the tomb says, 'He is not here'; another tells them to go to Galilee, there they will see him. He appears all over the place and just as quickly disappears. For Mary he is the gardener; for Cleophas and his friend he is the stranger. We begin to realise that, although this is the 'same Jesus Christ, yesterday, today and forever', he hasn't come back to earth simply to carry on where he had left off. That would obliterate entirely the wounds of the crucifixion and reduce Calvary to a mere hitch in the plan. Two things, then, (apart from witnessing to the Resurrection) are clear: we must learn to see Jesus and expect to meet up with him in constantly new ways. And secondly, the Cross wasn't a mistake; it was intended and we must always be ready for the cross whenever and however it may come our way. If we fail, we've failed to understand the Paschal Mystery.

The Emmaus incident (Lk 13–35) sheds considerable light on this. The first thing that strikes you is the fact that the two men are travelling away from Jerusalem. They are facing the wrong way. They are assuming that the Jesus event is over and they might as well go back and get on with their lives. The words, 'We had hoped,' say it all.

There is a curious parallel here to the infancy narratives, in which the parents of Jesus have gone a whole day's journey from Jerusalem, leaving Jesus behind in the Temple. This is also a story of departure and return, a fruitless journey made because they had failed to understand the *necessity* for Jesus to be in Jerusalem: 'Did you not know that I *must* be in my Father's house.' In both cases there is a conversion experience, a turning again. In each instance, there is a deeper insight. For Mary and Joseph, the Jesus they find in the Temple is not the same Jesus they sought after. When they found him, it was not the Jesus they had lost, or rather, the Jesus they had lost showed himself to be much more than they could ever grasp.

The Jesus the two disciples found was not the Jesus they had lost; again, he was a lot more. The very fact that he vanished from their sight at the moment of the breaking of bread, the very moment when they recognised him, is sufficient to prove he was no longer in the same realm as he was before. Mary Magdalen was told: 'Do not cling to me Mary'! We, too, cling to our old ideas and have to keep revising and renewing our own relationship with him. We never find him quite as we expected, or in quite the way we expect.

One has to admire Luke's superb irony. Irony is the midway between truth and falsity, a step towards illumination. When Jesus asks them, 'What things?' (as if he didn't know!) he's not fibbing; he is drawing them on. They reply, 'Concerning Jesus of Nazareth'. They conclude their little summary with: 'Some of those who were with us went to the tomb, and found it just as the women had said; but him they did not see.' And neither did they! Are we any better?

I learnt at school that irony is something that the audience knows and the actors do not know. The child Jesus said to his parents: 'Did you not know I must be in my Father's house?' We know why Jesus had to be getting on with his Father's business. As yet, his parents did not – at the time, at any rate.

Luke cleverly balances the failure of the two disciples to recognise Jesus when they meet him and their recognition of him when he broke bread. 'Jesus himself drew near and went with them. But their eyes were kept from recognising him.' Whilst when they stopped at Emmaus, we are told, 'And their eyes were opened and they recognised him.' Ironically, all the time Jesus was walking with them and explaining the Scriptures they weren't aware of it, then as soon as they became aware of who he was, he vanished from their sight. And here's a strange thing: they have to plead with him to stay with them, something we all wish that Jesus would do: stay with us. Here again is the irony, Luke tells us: 'Jesus acted as if he were going further,' when *he* knew all the while he was going to stay with them. He knew that he would stay with us, his Church, and be remembered in the breaking of bread: 'Do this in remembrance of me' – but not in a visible way.

It is the Footprints story in a slightly different version. On the way out Jesus was walking with them and they did not know it; on the way back, he is not visibly walking; he is much more! He is in them: in his Eucharistic presence and through his Holy Spirit. In other words, his footprints are no longer visible for he is with us far more closely. 'I live, no longer I, but Christ lives within me.'

The Lord is my Shepherd

4th Sunday after Easter (1993)

As it is Good Shepherd Sunday, I can do no better than say a few words about the Good Shepherd Psalm 22(23). It is unfortunate that it has become associated with funerals. The implication is that it is for death. One reason for this are the words 'valley of death'. But that is a mistranslation. It should be 'valley of darkness'. The word 'death' does not occur.

No, this psalm is for us, in this world, in all the crises of my life, not just the final one. The Jews use this psalm at grace before meals. That's much more appropriate.

For today, I must confine myself to the first sentence and say a few words about that. There's more than enough to be going on with. The first words are the key to the rest. *The Lord is my shepherd* – in any case; until those words are true for you, nothing else applies.

Very often when teachers teach this psalm they use the five fingers to help learn the first line. The (thumb) Lord (index finger) is (middle finger) my (ring finger) shepherd (little finger).

The – using the definite article you are showing you mean there is only *one* Lord: *The* Lord. All the rest don't exist. Then, when you say Lord, you are making a declaration about who is *your* shepherd. *Who* is your shepherd? Allah? Confucious? No. The *Lord* is my shepherd. This is very significant. Many people in this life have different thoughts. Some say, 'I look after myself.' Others say, 'The trade union is my "shepherd".' Some of you may remember a clever parody of this psalm which began 'The trade union is my shepherd, there is nothing I shall want.' For others it is the welfare state who will see them through from the cradle to the grave. But for us, it is the Lord.

And by *Lord* we have to mean Our Lord, for he said: 'I am the good shepherd. And only those who acknowledge Jesus as Lord can say this psalm; Muslims can't; Buddhists can't; atheists can't. How can they, if they don't believe Jesus is the Lord?

Is – the middle finger, is very important, although in the hebrew it is simply 'The Lord my shepherd.' *Is*, however, brings it to this present moment, here and now. If you say, The Lord *is* my shepherd, you are admitting he's responsible for you. He is taking care of you. How often do I say to people, 'Why are you trying to sort this out yourself? It's his responsibility, not yours. Say to him, Lord this is too much for me, you've got to sort this out. You are my shepherd.' And he will. He loves to have trust placed in him.

My – the fourth, your ring finger. There is something appropriate about *my* coming on this finger, because it suggests something special, something personal, like marriage. There is a story told of two ministers who were on a hike through the mountains of Wales. On their way, they met a boy looking after the sheep. One of them pulled out his pocket Bible and read the Good Shepherd psalm to him; and taught him how to remember it on his fingers. Some years later, they were back in the same area. It was a hot day and they were thirsty, so they knocked at a cottage door and asked if they could buy a drink. Whilst she was putting on the kettle, they noticed a photograph on the mantlepiece. And they said to the woman, 'Why, that's the boy we met two years ago. Can we meet him again?' 'No', she said, 'he's dead'. 'Oh! What happened?' 'Well,' she said, 'there was a terrible blizzard and he fell down a ravine, and before he was found he had died. But you know, there was something very unusual about him. His right hand was clasping his ring finger so tightly that they couldn't prize it away.'

The Lord is *my* shepherd.

Good Shepherd and Model

4th Sunday after Easter (2008)

The Pope, in his encyclical *Spe salvi*, has drawn our attention to the early Church's use of the Shepherd and Philosopher as symbols on the tombs of Christian graves. In the gospel today Jesus identifies himself as the Shepherd and the gate of the sheepfold. He is the true Shepherd who has passed through death ahead of us, to lead his sheep, his followers, into the safety of the eternal pastures.

One of the reasons why we read the parables of Jesus and especially this Good Shepherd parable, when we come to worship, is so that we ask ourselves such questions as, '*Are* we looking at life and the world in the right way?' 'What do we think when we hear the evening news and read the daily papers? *Who* are the people we look up to and admire?' Today, there are many competing voices vying to take us in many directions, all offering to 'give us life and give it more abundantly'. Can we hear the voice of the Good Shepherd calling amid the din of this life?

A friend of mine was helping write out the diaries of the mother of a friend of hers. The mother recorded something that occurred when, as a twelve-year-old in the 1880s, she was taking the sheep back to the fields. On the way she asked a lad to watch them while she ran in to tell her mother what she was doing. Coming out she found he hadn't watched them and all her sheep were mingled up with his. He, in his panic, was trying to remember which was which. She gave him a good scolding but told him not to worry. She set off down the lane. Every one of her sheep withdrew from the others and followed her; she didn't need to say anything: she just walked ahead of them.

This is the trust, the bond, the tie that keeps us following the right Shepherd, even when much of the time we are all mixed up with other sheep. When our Shepherd leads the way, we are alert and ready. We need to be reminded of the Good Shepherd. Unless we keep seeing him, hearing him, listening to his voice, daily, we may be too distracted to follow him when he moves off. We may not hear his voice when he calls our name.

It is important to realise, as we ponder the Easter mystery during this time, that the gospels are not 'on the scene' reports of Jesus' life. The gospels were written forty to seventy years after his resurrection. This is perhaps far more important for us to be aware of than were we reading accounts written at the time. What the evangelists were writing was from an ever growing conviction that Jesus had risen seventy years before and their experience of his action in their community was more than enough proof of his presence and his being alive among them. More to the point, the words they wrote were indeed the words of Jesus speaking to them and to us. We can just imagine how that community seventy years on was coping with 'the voice of strangers', with 'thieves and robbers', with 'those who steal and slaughter and destroy'. Are we hearing the right voices in our own time?

In the book we are having read at dinner each day, called: *Journey into Islam*, the author travels the Muslim world with these three American students. They meet and interview a wide range of different Muslims. The one, key question they keep asking is: who are your role models, who are the Muslims you look up to and identify with in the Muslim world? It is the role models who call the tune whether it be men like Osama Bin Laden who stood for the more fanatical, extremist approach, or the more conciliatory types, like Benazir Bhutto or Muscharrif of Pakistan. In the West we are equally familiar with the same quest for people who seem to have 'life and have it more abundantly': sporting stars, televsion icons, tycoons: these are the role models of the young people of today. Jesus, however, came to give us an altogether different kind of life: the life of God, eternal life.

Jesus knows exactly where he is leading us. We follow Jesus because he suffered for us, 'bore *our* sins in his body on the tree', 'gone through the valley of death with *us*'. He takes *us* nowhere where *he* has not been before himself. 'I have come,' he says, 'that you may have life and have it more abundantly.' At the Last Supper he said: 'I, your Lord and Teacher, have just washed your feet. You, then, should wash one another's feet. I have given you an example, so that you will do just what I have done for you.' (Jn 13:14) St Paul told the Philippians: 'Brothers, keep on imitating me. Pay attention to those who follow the right example that we have set for you' (Phil 3:17). He goes on to remind them, with tears in his eyes, of the many whose lives make them enemies of Christ's death on the cross.

We need role models, people who encourage us and motivate us to follow the right path. On this Sunday, we look up to and at Jesus as our role model; we celebrate Jesus' care for us and the unfailing certainty that he will not leave us like sheep without a shepherd. We think of David's own trust in God; 'Along the right path he leads me' (Ps 22[3]). If we follow Jesus – the Way, the Truth and the Life – we are sure he will lead us to the green and restful pastures of eternal life.

Friendship Sunday

6th Sunday after Easter (1993)

Friendship must be one of the deepest and most natural instincts human beings have. With even young children, you will hear them referring to 'my friend'. The laws which determine these childhood friendships are a bit beyond our adult minds, but children understand them, for they will say: 'I've fallen out with my friend.' There doesn't appear to be any inconsistency in still being friends with someone you have fallen out with. It makes life simpler, doesn't it?

I think we ought to call this 'Friendship Sunday'. The readings for all three years are suited to the subject. Those for Year B are certainly spot on: 'As the Father has loved me, so I have loved you … A man can have no greater love than to lay down his life for his friends. You are my friends if you do what I command you.' (Jn 15:9–15) But today's gospel (Year A) has the same underlying message: 'If you love me you will keep my commandments … and anyone who loves me will be loved by my Father, and I shall love him and show myself to him.'

From what one can learn about David Koresh's sect at Waco (Texas), the whole business was built on intimidation and domination. You could never have spoken of his followers as friends. They were manipulated subjects living under a tyranny. But turn to the gospels and the message that comes across is completely the opposite. It starts with love: 'God so loved the world'; and is penetrated with love to the end. 'Greater love than this, no man has, that he lay down his life for his friends.' St Paul put it even more dramatically: 'A man may die for his friend but Jesus died for us when we were at enmity with God.'

There was, it is clear, a very intimate level of friendship between Jesus and the apostles. John was the one Jesus had a special love for. Peter affirmed love three times: 'Lord, you know that I love you.' Then, there was the family of Martha, Mary and Lazarus with which Jesus was on such good terms. But the most remarkable aspect of all this is that friendship with Jesus didn't end with his death. The story of Christianity is ultimately the story of the friends of Jesus.

Samuel Johnson made the oft-quoted remark: 'Man should always keep his friendships in good repair.' My father used to say, 'a machine is only as good as its maintenance'. To keep our friendship with Jesus in good order we will have to work at it. It doesn't just happen, no more than a machine will go on working, or, more to the point, a good marriage will continue to succeed. John Mills, the actor, once stated: 'One of the secrets that made my marriage last (he married Mary Hayley Bell in 1941 and they were married for sixty-four years) has been working at the relationship. We're both very romantic. I send notes to Mary and she sends notes to me – even at dinner parties, if we are separated.'

Why, then, is there this bit about 'if you love me you will keep my commandments'? That is the language of master and servant: 'Do this!' and you do it. 'Go there!' and you go there. Jesus ruled that meaning out: 'No longer do I call you servants ... I call you friends' (Jn 15:15). The answer to the enigma lies partly in the order in which the words are placed: 'If you love me' comes before 'keep my commandments'. Once you love someone, you'll instinctively be wanting to do what they want, even if it does go a bit against the grain of self-love. That is one of the principal ways of maintaining your friendship with Jesus in good order – doing what he wants.

And *order* is the key word. We don't keep his will, his word, his commands because it is commanded, but because he is our friend, our *best* friend. He will then come *first* in our order of loves. After all, it's not that we don't love Jesus, it's that we don't love him enough to put him first.

Possibly, it may have been clearer, to us, if he had not just said, 'commandments', but 'the demands of love and friendship'. Friendship is not like something you can buy across the counter. It is like the air we breathe. You can't see it, or feel it. But you'd miss it if it weren't there. So it is with our relationship with Jesus if it's not one of friendship. If that is not there then faith and obedience – the two lungs – simply collapse. They can't function. Friendship is the very air they breathe.

A new relationship

7ᵗʰ Sunday after Easter (1981)

The Ascension marks the end of the period after the Resurrection during which Jesus appeared to the disciples to show them he had truly risen. But now that time has ended. Jesus was such an outstanding leader that his absence could have and would have spelt disaster for these men and women. But, he'd told them repeatedly, 'not to worry', he was going to send the Holy Spirit. So they all got together in the same room where Jesus had held the Last Supper, and – as we read in the first reading – 'all these joined in continuous prayer, together with several women, including Mary the mother of Jesus' – to prepare themselves for the coming of the Spirit.

They had two links with Jesus. They were in the same room where he had shared the Passover meal with them. And his Mum was there. She was praying with them. It 'kinda' makes it all much more homely. I was thinking isn't this a picture of what we are all doing here today? We have all come together to pray and prepare ourselves for this mysterious gift of his Holy Spirit, that Jesus has promised to send to look after us while he is away preparing a place for us.

What does it mean to receive the Holy Spirit? We hear a lot about the various gifts of the Spirit, but the first gift is simply the gift of God's love in our hearts. Love may be confused with lust but we all know the transforming effect it has on two peoples' minds and hearts and lives. So when we say the Holy Spirit is God's love poured into our hearts, then we can expect it to have a transforming effect in some ways. You may remember when Pope John Paul II visited Ireland, how at the conclusion of his talk to the youth of Ireland, he said 'Young people of Ireland, I love you.' It was inspiring to see the impact of those words.

Those three little words: *I love you* – how hard they are to say to someone, even those who mean everything to us, and yet how vital it is that we do say them. I remember a story told by Fr John Powell, an American Jesuit. After speaking about the importance in life of saying to our dear ones how much they mean to you, a woman came up to him and told him about her own experience of this. Their own fifteen-year-old son had just died. That evening she had gone to bed and called out to her husband to come too. He said he'd be up in a moment. But he didn't come so she went down to see what was the matter. He was just finishing writing a letter. This is what he wrote:

Dear boy,
I never told you how much I loved you; I never told you what a large part of my heart you occupied; I never told you what a large part in my life you played. I always thought there would be a right moment when I could tell you all these things – when you left school, when you went away to college, when you got married – there would be a right moment, then I could tell you all you meant to me and now you're gone and there never will be a right moment. And I do hope that God will let you see these words wherever you are.
Your loving Dad.

It's a moving little story, but it brings out what God has done in sending us his Holy Spirit. He is saying to us 'I love you'. It's a risk. Jesus found that out. But what would life be if we had never heard those words from God and had them shown in this, God's best gift to us, His Spirit?

It's the presence of God's love in our hearts that transforms our relationship to God. Before the Holy Spirit was poured into our hearts we couldn't even address God. But now, thanks to Jesus sending Him to us, we can call God, 'Our Father'. St Paul states this very clearly in Rom 8, v. 15:

For the Spirit that God has given you does not make you slaves and cause you to be afraid; instead, the Spirit makes you God's children, and by the Spirit's power we cry out to God, 'Father! My Father!' God's spirit joins himself to our spirits to declare that we are God's children.

Another text puts it even more beautifully: 'See what love the Father has given us that we should be called children of God, and so we are.'

During this week before Pentecost, and especially during this Mass, let us try to join with Mary and the disciples in praying and preparing ourselves for this great gift of God's Spirit and to hear God saying to us: *I love you.*

A cloud hid him

7ᵗʰ Sunday after Easter (2005)

On Thursday we celebrated the feast of the Ascension. St Luke tells us, Jesus, 'was taken up from before their very eyes, and a cloud hid him from their sight' (Acts 1:9). It's not surprising the angel had to bring the apostles down to earth as they remained there staring, and wondering what had happened to him. Did he become a kind of human space rocket, zooming off to heaven, like the Office Assistant on the computer when it whizzes away – heaven knows where? Whatever it was Luke draws the curtain of a cloud across the scene. The Bible consistently bears witness to two spheres of existence, the heavenly and the earthly. They are separate yet linked, and there are times in human experience where the 'join' is especially apparent. The Ascension is one of those moments.

Today's Mass acts as a bridge between the Ascension and Pentecost, between Jesus' going and his coming in the Spirit. The disciples on the way to Emmaus were heading in the wrong direction and Jesus had to point them along the right road. Similarly on this occasion, the disciples were staring up to heaven and the two angels had to bring them back to earth and tell them to get on with preparing the way for Jesus' return. It is natural for us to be intrigued by the mechanics of the Ascension, by what exactly happened to Our Lord, and all Luke tells us was that a cloud hid him. Luke is concerned about getting another message across. When they asked, 'Lord, are you at this time going to restore the kingdom of Israel?' they were hoping that the time had come at last for *heaven on earth*. They had got it wrong.

How many times have we been convinced of something only to find we were wrong? This then is the context in which we must read today's gospel. We all have a false idea of what heaven is going to be like – clouds, angels, harps, endless fine weather – and it is not surprising that many people, if pressed, would say that they find the whole idea rather boring. I sometimes think a good travel agent could paint a more attractive picture of heaven than what many of us imagine it to be like.

In today's gospel Jesus gives us a rare and rather mysterious indication of what heaven is like. He describes eternal life not in terms of where it is, of its location, but of the amazing reality of its nature, of what it is. 'Eternal life is this: to know you, the only true God, and Jesus Christ whom you have sent.' When we try to imagine heaven we try to imagine our dream world and then get frightened by the prospect of it having no end. That's because we can't get the idea of time out of our heads – and out of our idea of heaven. All our thinking is rooted in time and place. This is where we have got to 'think it out again', 'review the situation'.

Jesus, however, tells us that our eternal destiny is not rooted in a place, or in any particular activity, or in time, but in a relationship – a relationship of love.

There's another thing we keep getting wrong and which Jesus keeps telling us about. Eternal life doesn't start when we die, when time ends, so to speak, but rather it begins here and now, if we want it to. 'Eternal life is this: to know you, the only true God, and Jesus Christ whom you have sent.' (Jn 17:3) The 'join', I mentioned earlier between heaven and earth, is not only between two places, two experiences, it is between two phases, as it were: between the present phase: now / already and the next phase: the 'life of the world to come'. We already know, love and serve God. That is what the Catechism taught us: 'Why did God make you?' 'God made me to know him, love him and serve him in this world, and to be happy with him in this world and forever in the next.'

The fact that eternal life is not something that only begins when we die is brought out whenever Jesus speaks of the Eucharist. 'He who eats my flesh and drinks my blood *has* eternal life.' 'I have come that you may have life and have it more abundantly.' Just where the join is no one can say. St Paul speaks in one breath of the 'age to come', 'the glory yet to be revealed', and in the next breath speaks of it as already happening. It arrived on Easter day, with the risen Christ. It was made manifest at Pentecost. 'The life you have is hidden with Christ in God. But when Christ is revealed – and he is your life – you too will be revealed in all your glory with him' (Col 3:3–4).

Therein lies the message of today's readings: whilst we may be looking heavenward with the disciples, we must *come back to earth*, this earth and set to praying and working to bring about *heaven on earth*, even as Jesus is praying for us in this gospel.

I pray for them: I am not praying for the world but for those you have given me, because they belong to you: all I have is yours and all you have is mine, and in them I am glorified. I am not in the world any longer, but they are in the world, and I am coming to you.

CLOSING PRAYER

Lord, help us to live this day in the truth of your love for us. Help us to experience eternal life a little more each day by growing in our knowledge and love of you, for eternal life is to know your love and knowledge of us.

Gift of humour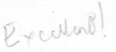

7th Sunday after Easter (1984)

There is one thing we all associate with the Holy Spirit and that is the gifts it brings. He himself is the Gift of God; God's first gift to us. Then, there are the familiar gifts of charity, joy, peace patience, wisdom and understanding. But there are also less familiar, less obvious gifts. The gift of humour, for instance. Humour and laughter are God's gifts to us and life would be a sorry business without them. But I thought it might pay to examine this gift a little for there is a wrong and a right way of using it.

Animals never laugh. They can't see the funny side. Laughter is human; it comes from surprise, from unexpected turns at the end of a joke, from playing on the meaning of words – or even the meaningless words: 'Get out of that' or 'You can't see the join'.

Just as we need comedians to make us laugh, we ourselves need a sense of humour to see the joke. Not everyone has the same sense of humour. Nor is someone always in a good mood and ready to see the funny side of life, especially if the joke is on us. No one likes being made a fool of. 'Don't laugh. It's not funny. You wouldn't like it.' Jokes can fall flat. Besides, there are times and places in life when humour is out of place. Pope John XXIII's last words: 'cheer up'. At other times, however, we need humour, we need our comedians, to put us in the mood, to get us out of despondency, and so to begin to see the funny side of things again.

We laugh and make fun of all kinds of different things. Where would life be without teasing and banter? We can say so much to others this way without hurting them. But sometimes we can take it too far, especially with children, for then we sometimes tease for entertainment, to make them angry.

It's the same with jokes. The thing is some jokes are in good taste and others are not. Some jokes are clean, some are vulgar. Like all God's gifts, humour can be abused. All too often these days, sex has become the pivot of so many jokes. Some are very clever and very funny, but somehow we must retain our ability to judge when a joke has gone too far and be able to say with Queen Victoria: 'We are not amused.' We've got to be able to make the switch back to real life and say, 'Joking apart ...'

Easier said than done. It's not easy to treat serious matters lightly without ending up treating them with derision. It's not easy to tease and make fun of other people's weaknesses and mistakes and not end up speaking unkindly and unfairly of them.

This brings me to the question of trivialisation. The great danger with the media is their tendency to trivialise everything. They make fun of all we hold most precious – sex, religion, politics, family life, etc. Life is heavy going at times, and we do become worried and overanxious about the future. Comedians and people with a sense of fun do us a power of good by helping us see the funny side of things, giving us a good laugh. We begin to love life again. When we can see the funny side we can also see the lovable side too. This applies to ourselves as well. It is a good rule to laugh at yourself once a day.

But fun can easily slip over into ridicule. It can make serious things seem trivial and not worth doing. Cardinal Hume, in *Searching for God,* points out the need to know which things to treat seriously and which to treat lightly. Sins, dishonesty, lying, immorality, etc. are serious matters, however much the media seem to treat them lightly. Other things such as social standing, popularity, clothes, wealth are not vital even if the media would have us think they are.

I could go on, but I've said enough to show that we ought to take our humour seriously. 'If you've got the faith you're laughing; if you're not laughing you've not got the faith!'

'Receive the holy spirit'

Feast of Pentecost (1993)

St Augustine wrote: 'Perfection consists not in what we give to God, but in what we receive from *Him*.' That connects in with something I read recently: 'We need to increase our expectancy of what God can do for us.' On this feast of Pentecost and the coming of the Holy Spirit, it seems one of the major obstacles to growth in the Spirit is our reluctance to open ourselves to his work within us.

Prayer is one area where most of us would like to see some improvement. We long to surrender ourselves and our lives to God; we ask him: 'Lord, what can I give?' And to our surprise, God replies, 'First you must learn to receive.' God is pouring out his love, and because we are so full of what we must do, it goes to waste. To catch God's love we have to empty ourselves.

Prayer is first and foremost learning to receive God's love. The very word 'pour' is significant because it is used often in connection with the Spirit. It's an image that's easy to grasp. I once was emptying the dregs of heating oil from a tank that was leaking. The bit turned out to be 25 gallons. My problem was finding the empty drums to pour it into. It gave me lots of practice in pouring. So when it says in Scripture words like: 'I will pour out my Spirit on all people' (Acts 2:17) or 'God has poured out his love into our hearts by means of the Holy Spirit, who is God's gift to us' (Rom 5:5), we begin to see what is required of us. Prayer is learning to receive, to open our hearts, to make space in them. Our Lady made space in her womb in order to receive the child that was conceived of the Holy Spirit. St Paul gives an added reason why we need to receive the Spirit especially when it comes to prayer.

> The Spirit comes to the help of our weakness. For we do not know how we ought to pray; the Spirit himself pleads for us in groans that words cannot express. And God who sees into our hearts, knows what the thought of the Spirit is (Rom 8:26).

Not only does the Holy Spirit act as our interpreter and 'go-between' with God. Without him we cannot even say Our Father, or Lord. In the second reading, St Paul reminds us: 'No one can say, "Jesus is Lord" unless he is under the influence of the Holy Spirit' (1 Cor 12:3).

And, to the Romans, St Paul says: 'The Spirit that God has given you ... makes you children of God, and by the Spirit's power we cry out to God, "Father, my Father!" God's Spirit joins himself to our spirits to declare that we are children of God' (Rom 8:15).

It need hardly be added that when I speak of the Holy Spirit I mean God's love. That's what we receive into our hearts. And in the conclusion to that Chapter 8 of Romans, Paul reaches the highest point of his doctrine on the Spirit:

> Who can separate us from the *love* of God? Can trouble do it, or hardship? ... No in all these things we have complete victory through him who loved us. I am certain that nothing can separate us from his love.

That, then, is why it is so important to receive and accept God's love into our hearts.

God's Hiddenness

4th Sunday after Pentecost (1969)

> *Truly ours is a hidden God (Isa 45:15).*

If there is one reason why modern man gets less and less interested in religion, it is because God is hidden from us. At least he is not scientifically discoverable. And with scientists so confidently and so rapidly mastering the mysteries of this world and uncovering its hidden secrets, people are becoming more sceptical about God as science reveals nothing about him.

Not so long ago, the Russians sent a rocket to Venus. They obtained all kinds of information from the signals it sent back. But, apparently – so the story goes – 'they found no trace of God out there in space'. That does not surprise us. We know God is a spirit and does not live in any particular place which, provided you go on looking for long enough, you will find. After all, their argument is: there were ships on the Atlantic long before America was found though it existed all the time, and no one knew it. It was the same with the atom; the only reason we did not know about it was because we hadn't the instruments to detect it. Strange to say, what would have surprised us would have been to hear that the Russians *had* discovered God's dwelling place in outer space. They didn't, and we know they never shall. God will always remain beyond the reach of human senses and outside the world of 3D. The God we believe in and worship is a hidden God.

We know this well enough. Even so, it is difficult not to be disconcerted by the fact that *our* knowledge of God isn't growing at the same pace as the scientist's knowledge of the world. It is a fact, however, we must turn around and face. Unless we admit to the reality that our religious knowledge of God is not the same as our knowledge of this earth, we may easily find ourselves becoming dissatisfied with the Church, saying, 'it's not keeping up with the times'.

One way of avoiding this pitfall is to keep constantly in mind the truth that our God is hidden. To appreciate more this simple and obvious truth we must look back rather than forward.

God's hiddenness runs through scripture. First there is the fundamental axiom: 'No man can see God and live.' God is a spirit and invisible to the human eye. In the book of Exodus, Moses pleaded with God to show him his face, and God said, 'I will let my splendour pass in front of you, and I will pronounce before you the name Yahweh ... you cannot see my face, though, for no man can see me and live.' And Yahweh said, 'Here is a place beside me ... when my glory passes by I will ... shield you with my hand while I pass by. Then I will take my hand away and you shall see the back of me; but my face is not to be seen.' Only those who have died can enjoy this privilege of seeing God.

God is hidden not only in himself, but also in his ways. And these can be even more perplexing since they never seem to line up with our ways of thinking. Yet, as God himself says in scripture: 'As the sky is as far from the earth so are my ways from your ways.' And again: 'I have compassion on whom I will and I show pity to whom I please.' (Ex 34:21) If you try to analyse some of God's choices and preferences in the Bible, you will end up in despair. Why did he choose Israel in the first place? Egypt was a far greater and more civilised country. So were Babylon and Assyria. We can ask the same question about the time and place of the Incarnation. Why did Christ spend thirty years hidden in the obscurity of a small provincial country like Palestine? Nobody can fathom God's ways. It is a mystery why God favours one man and rejects another. Why God at one moment is near and deeply concerned, then, the next moment he is far away and his people are afflicted with war, pestilence and famine.

It is because of God's hiddenness that men have invariably failed to recognise him. God complains of this to Osee (to take one of many examples), and refers to himself as a jilted lover: 'God said to Osee, give your love to a woman, loved by her husband but an adulteress in spite of it, just as Yahweh gives his love to the sons of Israel though they turn to other gods.' (3:1) We meet the same lack of understanding and reasons in the New Testament. Our Lord asked: 'How often would I have gathered you together like a hen gathers her chickens and you would not?' Christ was God present on earth, but because his divinity was hidden, he went unrecognised. The onlookers at Calvary jeered: 'If thou be the Son of God come down from the cross and we will believe.' And then, a short while after, some realised their mistake and cried out in dismay: 'Indeed this was the Son of God.'

Even from this very sketchy outline, you can see what a very profound mystery we are up against. Nor must we be surprised if this is how our religion appears to us. Our Lord warned us of just this in so many of his parables: The Five Wise and the Five Unwise Virgins. When the bridegroom had gone in with the five wise virgins and the others came along late asking to be admitted, the Lord answered: 'I know you not.' They had missed their chance. Then, there is the famous parable of the sheep and the goats. Both the sheep and the goats asked: 'Lord, *when* did we see thee sick and imprisoned ... *when* did we see thee hungry and thirsty.' It was exactly the same for the sheep as for the goats. The Lord was as hidden from the sheep as from the goats. And so it is with us. More often than not we experience God's absence rather than his presence. And yet in spite of it our knowledge and love are growing imperceptively all the time. You have only to think of the ideas and images of God you had as a child to see how you have progressed. The fact that we do not expect to find God in outer space shows we know God is a spirit who does not live in time or space and cannot be seen with the human eye, aided or not.

It is interesting to notice how we experience a similar kind of hiddenness in our relations with others – friends, partners in marriage, parents too and children. No matter how devoted, how dedicated and united two people may be, there will always remain an area which is hidden from the other and which cannot be shared. There is something in each of us which belongs to God alone and which we can only share with him. It makes us feel sad at times that this should be so, one is so anxious to be completely open with people we love. But, if this hidden area belongs to God, then we must reverence and respect it as God's. They have to do the same for us. And maybe – I'm only guessing here – this is a lesson God wants us to learn. *He* has shown us how much he loves us and wants to be united with us, but at the same time he knows there will be part of himself he can never share with us, even in heaven. So if we learn to live with this in this life we shall not be disappointed in the next.

This subject of God's hiddenness is unending. All I can say in conclusion is to remind you of a well-known prayer that can be used on so many occasions: 'Hidden God, devoutly I adore you.'

God's Silence

5th Sunday after Pentecost (1969)

Last time I was talking about God's hiddenness both in himself and in his ways. Today, I thought it would be interesting to think about God's silence. His silence is not quite the same as his hiddenness. They are connected. They both make a considerable difference to prayer, as well as to our religion in general. The fact that God is *hidden* makes it difficult to address ourselves to him. That need not be an insuperable obstacle; after all, the person at the other end of the phone is hidden, so is the speaker on the radio. It is because God is *silent* and never replies audibly that makes our prayer seem such an empty echo of our thoughts and words.

Not for a moment am I questioning the undoubted fact that God has spoken to us in the past through the prophets, and even spoke to us himself in the person of his Son, Jesus Christ. It also goes without saying that we are listening to God speaking whenever we hear the Scriptures read – these we call 'God's Word'. And also, whenever the Church speaks on fundamental questions, this is another occasion and another way in which God speaks to us. All this I am taking for granted, important though it is. Unfortunately it doesn't alter the actual silence of God each of us experiences in our private and individual lives and prayers. Our best efforts at prayer, instead of being the intimate conversation between father and child we would like them to be, are usually more of a dreary monologue with our voice sounding far too much. There are and have been exceptional people, the mystics. These seem to have had a 'private line', as it were – or judging from their levitations, their ecstasies and their visions they did. That type of person, however, is hardly normal.

God's silence does present us with a dilemma. Because God is silent, does that mean we are to be silent in return, and therefore are excused from trying to pray? This is the conclusion the world draws from God's silence. This is why they cannot understand churchgoers. Very often they believe in the *existence* of a supreme being, but they can't see the reason for praying to someone who never replies, who doesn't seem to care and who wouldn't be bothered if the world blew itself up. The Church, on the other hand, draws exactly the opposite conclusion, and constantly upholds the value and advantage of praying to God in spite of the silence. She teaches us that God is not a helpless spectator on the touchline unable to do anything. He is in control of this world and includes our prayers in his government of it. We all know this very well; still, it doesn't alter the silence and this is where we are torn between the world on one side arguing the futility of it all. It's trump card is God's silence – 'Have you ever heard him speak' they say, in effect. On the other side, there is the Church. She is far from silent; she goes to great lengths to show us how God speaks to us in many and various ways: through the events of our lives, through the wonders of creation, and above all through other men.

Let us consider a bit more the world's silence about God. For the most part it rather tends to ignore God. One does not hear much about God in industry or the world of sport. Cinema and television, newspapers and magazines also keep pretty quiet about him. Only very rarely does an article or a programme, such as the current one *Reason to Believe*, or a film, such as *A Man for all seasons*, allow itself to be involved in this age-old debate about God's silence and the conclusions we are meant to draw from it. Robert Bolt's play and the film about Thomas More present God's silence as the biggest decision that can face a man. Here was a man who was prepared to let go of his position, his reputation, his family, and even his own life. He had to choose between the silence of God and all the opposition of a very vocal world. True, he had the example of Our Lord and many holy martyrs. Yet I doubt whether he received a personal message from God to confirm him in his choice. God's silence, then, is the supreme trial and condition of real faith. And such films admit it.

At this point, we must digress a little, and ask ourselves what do we look to the Church for? Why do we come to Church? Why do we attend Mass? Is it because belonging to the Church gives us a feeling of solidarity? Is it because she has been so long established and has such a great tradition? Perhaps we value the Church for her various organisations, because she puts up fine buildings and performs splendid ceremonies full of pageantry. We might even consider her worthwhile belonging to because she is a good spiritual United Nations and more effective than any other contemporary body at remedying present evils. The Church is all those, but she is also something else. We come to Church and stay in the Church because we are searching for God and she helps us in this search much more than the world. We come to our Mother the Church as the disciples came to Our Lord and said, 'Master, teach us how to pray.' The Pope pointed out recently in an address, that the Church's main function is to teach us how to pray to God. She teaches us not only how to pray, but what things to pray for, who to pray *for* – the dead as well as the living, and who to pray *to* – the saints. She not only teaches us this, she does it with us in the Mass. The Mass is the most perfect prayer.

Prayer is no more than learning how to express ourselves before God in truth and love. A child has to learn the same lessons in regard to his elders as we have to learn in regard to God our Father. A child has to be taught to say, 'yes, please'; 'no, thank you'; 'sorry'; or 'excuse me'. He has to learn how to address people and how to express himself civilly and humanly. And it is the same with prayer. We learn to make acts of gratitude and sorrow. To ask for favours. There is one great difference. Prayer requires faith for we are always up against God's silence. We are, as it were, forever speaking into a phone, in which God, at the other end, can hear but does not speak back.

There are lots of conclusions one could draw from such a topic as this. The title of a recent book about the contemplative life sums up very well what I've been attempting to say: it is called *Against all Reason*. In a sense, it is against all reason – worldly reason at any rate – that we believe in things like prayer. It is against all reason that we plunge ourselves and our lives into this silence of God, that we entrust ourselves to him. Even if we do get no self-evident reply and plenty of discouragement from an incredulous world, we will still go on offering up to him our prayers, works and sufferings and our whole lives, trusting he sees and hears all. We will also take whatever the Church says as coming from him, for he said: 'He who hears you, hears me.'

Prayer

Sunday after Corpus Christi (1969)

As prayer plays such an essential part in our lives as Catholics, I've tried to put a few thoughts together on various aspects of this subject. There is no limit to what I could say; there is a definite limit to what I can say, partly because of the time limit and partly because of my own limited knowledge. In many ways, the Church is a 'limited company'. She does her best, but it is within limits.

Most of us know perfectly well that prayer of petition is not the only kind of prayer. But it is the prayer we seem best at, simply because there is never any shortage of things to be asked for. There is a real problem here. Why doesn't God give us all we need (and that goes for the world as well)? There is so much to ask for that we never get on to other kinds of prayer. The answer to this problem is that prayer of petition is not a device for obtaining things we've failed to get any other way. Some people think of prayer in terms of refuelling at a garage. You pull up to the station, ask for ten gallons and expect to leave with the needle of the gauge registering 'full'. It would certainly free our minds and enable us to pass on to other forms of prayer *if* we could have all our needs answered as easily as that. We could then sit back and say to ourselves: 'I shall not have to worry about petrol for a bit.' This is not how *God* works, or how *prayer* works. Has God ever given us more than enough? And yet, has there ever been a time when we haven't had enough?

A further way of illustrating this question is to think of our lives as a bath full of water without a plug to stop the water running out. The water of our lives is running out all the time. Try as we might, we cannot block up that hole. And when all our money and natural efforts have proved useless we rush to the taps of prayer hoping God will fill us up to the point of overflow. But as he barely gives us enough even to keep the level up we rush back to the plug again. The point of both these examples is this: prayer of petition is not supposed to get God to do my will, but enable me to do God's will, to dispose me to accept whatever God wills. It gives me the confidence to trust God to maintain enough water in the bath to keep me afloat, enough petrol in the engine to keep me going.

Prayer of petition, then, especially before the Blessed Sacrament, is not so much a begging prayer as a trusting prayer. And straightaway one begins to see why so many people misunderstand it and don't feel it is any use, above all when it fails to bring what they asked for. They treat prayer as little more than a slot machine for getting something they were unable to get by other means. They look upon God as a reserve water tank to be used only in time of need. I'm not suggesting we must not pray for ourselves and for our salvation, we must; but we must not pray on an 'I-pray-you-give' basis.

The way to get around the dilemma is not to come to prayer hoping to receive, but to come intending to give, to entrust ourselves, our families, our lives to God our Father. We *give up* to him all we want rather than ask for it, and accept only what he wants. This prayer of trust is like a pair of *scales*: God on one side and myself on the other. I come into church with my side weighed down with a list of requirements as long as your arm – every one labelled urgent, please reply quickly, first class mail, if possible, whilst God's side is dangling up in the air empty. What I have to try and do is not weigh God's side to my level, but unload my side until it reaches God's level. I've got to take each thing off, one by one, and let it go. Gradually – the odd thing is – as my side gets lighter and begins to go up, God's instead of remaining in the same position, begins to come down. Whether the two scales eventually become level, and my side balances perfectly with God's, will depend on the extent to which I can give up and let go of all my needs.

Isn't this the kind of prayer Christ prayed in the garden? Isn't this what our Lord meant when he said: 'Come to me all you who are burdened and I will refresh you' (Mt 11:28)? This giving-up prayer is wonderfully lightening and refreshing. *But it comes at a cost*. It is so hard to let go of our needs and to accept what God wants. It is not easy to entrust them to the Lord. Any parent, a mother especially, does not readily let go of a son or a daughter and entrust them to someone else – another teacher, or to a husband or wife, or even to the Lord in the religious life. Yet they have to because life cannot go on without this trust.

It is at prayer that we achieve this quiet, trusting attitude. Sometimes, all this giving-up may go on in the inner reaches of our souls. All we can do is kneel there and even give up the desire to be able to express ourselves as we should have liked. Yet the very fact of wanting to pray, wanting to trust God, is often the best and only way of praying. The test of whether the desire is genuine is whether we can drop all those other things we usually find to do and go and spend some time on our knees in church.

On a number of occasions in our Lord's life, he used the words 'fear not; it is I'. Why did he use these words so often? I think we have all experienced this kind of fear. We must have had it at school sometimes when called to the headmaster's room. We may even get it now, occasionally, when the telephone rings, or when someone unexpected knocks at the door. Apprehensively we pick up the receiver and say 'who's there?' and we are immensely relieved to hear the reassuring reply, 'it's me'. Well, prayer before the Blessed Sacrament is not unlike that. We come into church with fears, anxieties and worries ringing in our minds and banging on the door of our hearts and we open them to the Lord. And he replies, 'fear not, *it* is I'. The *it*, whoever or whatever 'it' is, is the *what* our Lord wants. And so we say: 'Oh, it's you Lord, after all, thank God for that. That's all I really want.' But if we hadn't prayed about it we would never have recognised it and never accepted it as coming from our Lord.

Who are you?

2nd Sunday, Ordinary Time (1990)

A woman was in a coma and dying. Suddenly she had a feeling that she was taken up to heaven and was standing before the Judgement Seat. 'Who are you?' a voice said to her. 'I'm the wife of the mayor,' she replied. 'I did not ask whose wife you are but who you are.' 'I'm the mother of four children.' 'I did not ask whose mother you are but who you are.' 'I'm a schoolteacher.' 'I did not ask what your profession is but who you are.' And so it went on. No matter what she replied, she did not seem to give a satisfactory answer to the question, 'Who are *you*?'. 'I'm a Christian.' 'I did not ask what your religion is but who you are.' 'I'm the one who went to church every day and always helped the poor and needy.' 'I did not ask what you did but who you are.' She evidently failed the examination, for she was sent back to earth. When she recovered from her illness, she was determined to find out who she was. And that made all the difference [from *Taking Flight*, by Anthony de Mello, p. 140, 'The Self'].

The question 'Who are you?' was always much to the fore in the life of Jesus. Even the Angel Gabriel was trying to tell Our Lady who Jesus was to be: 'He will be great; he will be the Son of David; he will save his people from their sins; you shall call him Jesus.'

There can scarcely be a single page of the gospel in which this question of the identity of Jesus doesn't come up in one way or another. Jesus goes to great pains to try and answer it. In St John's gospel he gives nine answers. On nine occasions he uses the words '*I am*': 'I am the Good Shepherd', 'I am the Way, the Truth, and the Life', 'I am the Vine'; 'I am the Door', and so on.

In today's gospel we have John the Baptist telling his followers who Jesus is: 'Seeing Jesus coming towards him, John said, "Look, there is the Lamb of God who takes away the sin of the world."'

Of all the answers supplied, to liken Jesus to a lamb seems about the most unlikely. 'Like a little child', yes; or, 'like a roaring lion' or a 'thundering bull', but like a lamb! A lamb is the gentlest of all animals, a picture of helplessness and innocence. Isaiah will describe him as 'like a lamb that is led to the slaughter'. We can even go back to Exodus where the paschal lamb's blood was sprinkled on the doorposts to save the Israelites from the avenging angel.

And many of those who came to know Jesus in the gospels knew him as the one who had taken away their sin. Indeed, they would settle for nothing less – Jesus has taken away my sin. Cripples, prostitutes, tax collectors, thieves, they all received individual attention. Even his executioners had their guilt taken away. 'Father, forgive them! They don't know what they are doing' (Lk 23:24).

The difference in the executioners' case from the others was that they didn't know they were forgiven. They couldn't experience forgiveness in the same way as Zaccheus could the day 'salvation came to his house'.

Without knowing who Jesus is you can't know *who you are*. Mary Magdalen was identified as 'she who had seven devils driven out of her'. We are identified as sinners – forgiven sinners. Jesus is the one who has saved me from my sins.

The words 'Jesus, Lamb of God' are woven into the Mass (and have been since the 8th century). When the priest holds up the host and says: 'Behold the Lamb of God, behold him who takes away the sin of the world', he adds: 'Blessed are those called to the supper of the Lamb.' To know you are a sinner, to know you are a forgiven sinner and are called to share in the feast of the Lamb is to be truly happy (Rev 19).

Here I am, Lord

2nd Sunday, Ordinary Time (2005)

Y ou've got to admire John. Here is a man of whom Jesus exclaimed: 'Among those born of women there has risen no greater than John the Baptist' (Mt 11:11). Jesus was really handing it to John for accomplishing exactly what he was asked to do – pave the way for Jesus. Yet John did not regard Jesus as a threat to his job. There's no envy or jealousy in John. Envy and jealousy: *there's* a thought to start the year off with! Am I, or are you, jealous or envious?

If you weren't you wouldn't be human. If you don't think you *are* occasionally then you may need to think again. Jealousy and envy are there on almost every other page of the bible. Adam and Eve were envious of God for having knowledge which they did not. Cain was envious of Abel because his sacrifice went down better than his. David was envious of Uriah the Hittite because of his wife Bathsheba. Saul was jealous of David. The Jewish authorities were envious of Jesus. Not just envious; they were jealous.

What, then, is the difference between envy and jealousy? St Thérèse recounts Aesop's fable on envy. The donkey in the farmyard envied the dog at the master's table, which he could see by looking through the back door into the farm kitchen. Every time the dog put his paw on the lap of someone he got some titbits. The donkey envied him and thought he'd give it a try. He barged into the kitchen, put his hoof on the table and tipped the whole table over. He was soundly thrashed for his trouble.

Envy is dissatisfaction with what belongs to you and coveting what belongs to another. Two out of the Ten Commandments deal with covetousness. Thou shalt not covet thy neighbour's goods and thou shalt not covet thy neighbour's wife. In a class about the Commandments, a young boy put up his hand and asked: 'Please, Miss, how can envy and jealousy be wrong if God was jealous?' 'Where does it say that?' she queried, playing for time. 'The First Commandment, Miss. "I, the Lord your God, am a jealous God."'

The answer to that one would be that God has no rivals. There is no other 'God'; he has the sole right to our worship. That leads into the first Commandment: you shall not make yourself an idol or bow down and worship them. It's only, *then*, a manner of speaking to say God is jealous. When we speak of human jealousy, we mean the fear that what is ours may be lost to another. King Saul was bitterly jealous of David. He was terribly afraid David was out to get his throne. He wasn't, but that didn't stop Saul thinking he was and being jealous. Henry VIII was eaten up by jealousy – and envy.

The two are so closely linked it's hard not to confuse them. Ours has been called '*the envious society*'. The pop idol, pop star, icon culture thrives because it feeds on people's envy. We envy people their looks, their possessions, their relationships, their seemingly exciting and exotic lives and wish we were in their place. Jealousy more especially robs people of their inner peace as they devise ways to eliminate the person *they think* is standing in the way to *their* personal fulfilment.

How utterly different John the Baptist was! How self-effacing:

> Here is the Lamb of God who takes away the sin of the world! This is he of whom I said, 'After me comes a man who ranks ahead of me because he was before me' (Jn 1:29–30).

Again he said: 'He must increase, but I must decrease' (Jn 3:30).

The question I asked myself was where does all this envy and jealousy inside us come from? First of all, it comes from a basic dissatisfaction we all feel within ourselves. Somehow everyone else seems to have more, and lead more exciting lives than we do. We might even think they are happier.

That is how it is. We come into this world with insatiable desires, huge talents, boundless energy and expectations, golden dreams. Without them there would be no progress. But because of fallen human nature, these perfectly natural desires and ambitions turn sour and turn into envy and jealousy of others.

The responsorial antiphon fits perfectly today. *Here I am, Lord*. This is where I am: in one particular town, in one particular job, with one particular partner, with one particular family, with one particular set of friends, and with one very concrete round of domestic duties and commitments. All our potential, all our desires, all our talents and ambitions have come down to this – this job, this place, this little corner, this little part in history. *Here I am, Lord*. It cannot but fail to fall short of our expectations. That is how easy it is for envy and jealousy to find a place in our hearts.

CLOSING THOUGHT

David Thoreau (the American author, poet and philosopher) once said, as a young person we dream of building a bridge to the moon and sometime in midlife we pick up the materials we've gathered and build a woodshed in the garden. It's not easy to be satisfied with a woodshed and to be stuck with that. That is why, the response today is just right. It is the secret to inner peace and contentment. More importantly the secret to our life of union with Jesus and his holy will. In his will lies our inner peace and strength.

Hope in him, hold firm

3rd Sunday, Ordinary Time (2008)

The people that walked in darkness have seen a great light; on those who live in a land of deep shadow a light has shone (Isa 9:2).

Matthew, with his Jewish people who knew Isaiah in mind, quotes this passage. For Matthew these words are prophetic and are fulfilled in the person of Jesus. The great light that Matthew himself had experienced shining through Jesus was recognised by Peter and the others who answered his call, but it is still something of an exception. The statistics in the columns of the papers about falling numbers of Mass-goers, baptisms and weddings is an indication of how the voice of progress, this world and its appeal speaks louder than the voice of Jesus. Unless we keep our eyes fixed on him we will lose sight of this ray of light and hope in these difficult times. The responsorial psalm was chosen because of the verse 'the *Lord* is my light and my help'. Psalm 26(27) from which the response is taken is full of promise, full of hope, ending as it does with the words: 'I am sure I shall see the *Lord's* goodness in the land of the living. Hope in *him*, hold firm and take heart. Hope in the *Lord.*'

Pope Benedict's new encyclical *Spe Salvi* is on hope. The present-day crisis of faith, Pope Benedict urges and argues, is a crisis of Christian hope. The abandonment of Christian hope in favour of faith in progress and technology is a road leading deeper into darkness. Hope for humanity is not in ideologies but in God who has loved us and sent his Son to us to be our light and our hope.

Spe salvi facti sumus – 'in hope we are saved' – the very opening words quoted from Romans are also addressed to us. Salvation is not a given. Redemption is offered by giving us a hope, a trustworthy hope, which enables us to live in the present and accept our lives as they are. We can take the hard and difficult things if we have hope. For example, someone who is ill with cancer will be prepared to undergo an operation because of the hope they have of being healed and healthy again. The goal has to be big enough to justify the means.

The Pope establishes the link between hope and salvation. He also explains how this link is virtually indistinguishable from faith. Our hope of eternity and beatitude is hope for something we cannot see or really know. It can only be known by faith, the gift of faith. The Pope then quickly reminds us how that hope without Jesus is nothing. St Paul puts this question to the Ephesians. What were they like before their encounter with Christ? They were like a people without hope. They grieved over their dead because they had no hope (Eph 2:12–14). The Pope reiterates: 'It is not that Christians know the details of what awaits them, but they know in general terms that their life will not end in emptiness.'

He then introduces the key distinction between 'informative' and 'performative' hope. Most people know vaguely about heaven and have even vaguer ideas of what it is – sitting on clouds, strumming harps forever. That sort of knowledge doesn't inspire anyone. What he means by performative is the effect it has on your life. It is life-changing. 'The dark door of the future has been thrown open. The one who hopes, lives differently; the one who hopes has been granted the gift of new life.' A friend was telling me of how once, when she was a child, knowing when the seaside holiday was going to be, she started saving to be able to buy the goodies she knew would be there. That's the performative sort of hope.

The Pope draws our attention to the life of St Josephine Bakhita in order to show exactly what it means. St Josephine came from Darfur in Sudan. At the age of nine she was kidnapped by slave traders and was abused and beaten for years by different owners. Then an Italian merchant bought her and her whole life changed. St Josephine came to know a completely different type of master. In so doing she also came to know another master, Jesus. He too had bought her (redeemed her). She began to realise what it was to be known and loved and that this master too had been flogged and was awaiting her 'at the Father's right hand'. 'The people that walked in darkness have seen a great light.'

Using the carvings on the graves of early Christians, the Pope shows how we learn what they were thinking when faced by death and the hereafter. One of the principal images is that of Christ as shepherd 'The Lord is my shepherd: I shall not want ... Even though I walk through the valley of the shadow of death, I fear no evil, because you are with me ...' (Psalm 22[23]:1, 4). The true shepherd is one who knows even the path that passes through the valley of death; one who walks with me even on the path of final solitude, where no one can accompany me, guiding me through: he himself has walked this path, he has descended into the kingdom of death, he has conquered death, and he has returned to accompany us now and to give us the certainty that, together with him, we can find a way through. The realisation that there is One who even in death accompanies me, and with his 'rod and his staff comforts me', means so that 'I fear no evil' (Psalm 22[23]) – this was the new hope that arose in the life of believers.

From this brief look at the Pope's latest encyclical we can see how well it expresses the hopes and expectations of the first disciples and why St Matthew should see in Jesus the great light that shone on the people who walked in darkness. 'Hope in *him*, hold firm and take heart. Hope in the *Lord*' (Ps 26).

If the salt loses its flavour

5th Sunday, Ordinary Time (1999)

You are the salt of the earth

S alt of the earth? What is Jesus trying to tell us? It's a compliment to start with. It's a phrase Jesus coined and has become part of our vocabulary.

However, as with so many things Jesus said, after the praise comes the condition. 'But if the salt becomes tasteless, what can make it salty again?' Salt is a vital ingredient of food. Without it, food becomes insipid. We lose our appetite for it.

Salt, however, presumes a sense of taste. What if we lose our taste, so that we can't taste whether it's sweet or sour? Taste is a key element in our lives. I don't know what your favourite cheese is. For me, on a special occasion, I like Danish Blue or Stilton. Just imagine if I lost my sense of taste and I could no longer taste that special flavour of the cheese. If food no longer tasted, we'd lose all interest in it.

Obviously, Our Lord is using salt and saltiness in a metaphorical sense when he says, 'You are the salt of the earth.' Not a simile: 'You are like the salt of the earth.' A metaphor is much stronger. Even so, it doesn't literally mean that we are salt. The message he wants to drive home is so like the case of salt and its properties that it brings it out better than any other example.

What's then is the point which Our Lord is trying to make? It's this: St Bernard explains that spiritual things have a taste, just like salt has. If spiritual things lose their taste then we are in trouble. We shall, as we say, have no taste, no appetite for them. I think you will agree this describes perfectly the trouble so many of our present generation find with going to church. They have lost their appetite for it. They have no taste for spiritual realities.

St Bernard, being the great Doctor of the Church he is, diagnoses the cause of the disease, he calls it *curiositas*, which is the latin for curiosity. People have lost their taste for things of the spirit, for religion, because they have an insatiable desire, hunger, curiosity for news of the world, for things of the flesh. It is the taste for these that has given them a distaste for the things of God. St Bernard observes how we are driven on by curiosity. We never seem to have enough of news, and the more ghastly and the more deviant the better. Like the man who exclaimed, somewhat wearily, after watching television all evening: 'I'll be glad when I've had enough.'

What's gone wrong? Why have we lost our taste? Why have so many people no desire, no appetite for spiritual things? What is more to the point, how are we to give people their taste back again? 'You are the salt of the earth. If the salt loses its taste and becomes tasteless, what can make it salty again?' (Mt 5:13) Jesus doesn't give us his answer which is a bit of a shame. However, we can be certain that he's saying it is up to us. It's up to us to be preservers of the Faith, up to us to be softeners where there is hardness, up to us to melt the coldness of others by our warmth, and above all give them a taste and an appetite for the Faith by our genuine and sincere love of it.

My mother often used to comment in her declining years how the church and things of the church were no longer the topic of conversation they used to be. She said, when she was young, the conversation seemed to centre on the feasts and the events at church. Now, it's only the bad news about people in the Church that are talked about.

A man cried out to Jesus in prayer: 'Lord, I have a problem.' 'What is it?' Jesus replied. 'It's me,' he said. 'In that case, I have the answer,' Jesus said, 'What is it?' the man answered eagerly. 'It's me,' Jesus said. St Bernard explains this in his own way. He says, that for him, if anything he is reading is not sweetened by the name of Jesus it leaves him cold. If you have Fr Paul's little book, *Love without Measure*, you'll find that famous passage of St Bernard in it. I quote:

> The name of Jesus is more than light, it is also food ... Every food of the mind is dry if it is not dipped in that oil; it is tasteless if not seasoned by that salt. Write what you will, I shall not relish it unless it tells of Jesus.

Talk or argue about what you will, I shall not relish it if you exclude the name of Jesus. Jesus to me is honey in the mouth, music in the ear, a song in the heart.

For St Bernard, what gives meaning and taste to his reading, or his listening to God's Word is the name of Jesus. With it, all is well; without it, all is tasteless and insipid. Similarly as St Paul said: 'During my stay with you, the only knowledge I claimed to have was about Jesus, and only about him as the crucified Christ.' Paul never tried to entertain his listeners with clever philosophies and so on. He relied on preaching Jesus and him crucified. That's what we've lost the taste for: the message of the Cross.

'You are the salt of the earth.' If you are not to lose your taste for the things of the spirit, then season all that you do and think with the name of Jesus. He is the way, the truth and the life. He is the one who will give us distaste for the news of the world and a love for the things that are above.

Power and influence

11th Sunday, Ordinary Time (1999)

L ast week the gospel was about the call of Matthew, the tax collector. This week we are told that Jesus was filled with compassion because the crowds were like sheep without a shepherd. How can he best influence them for the better? His first recommendation is to pray: the harvest is great the labourers are few. Then he calls his twelve.

Why did Jesus choose these ordinary men from ordinary careers and jobs? Were these to be the sort of people who would be able to influence and persuade people to his way of thinking? Why didn't he go to the priests and the Levites, to the learned? Surely, they would be more convincing, more persuasive? Though all of us here owe it ultimately to the apostles for the faith we received, we know extremely little about them, except that they were very ordinary people. As St Paul reminded the Corinthians:

> So then, where does that leave the wise? Or the scholars? Or the skilful debaters of this world? God has shown that this world's wisdom is foolishness … Now remember what you were when God called you. From the human point of view, few of you were wise or powerful or of high social standing. God chose what the world considers nonsense in order to shame the wise, and he chose what the world considers weak in order to shame the powerful. (1 Cor 1:20–27)

Paul is saying it is never due to human powers of persuasion that men and women turn to the Lord. It is the power of God at work in us.

St Paul leads us deeper into the secret of why Jesus chose such an average cross section of people. He says:

> When I came to you to preach God's secret truth, I did not use big words and great learning. For while I was with you, I made up my mind to forget everything except Jesus Christ and especially his death on the

cross. Your faith then, does not rest on human wisdom but on God's power (1 Cor 2:1–5).

It is clear that Jesus didn't want men who would preach themselves, and boast about the number of conversions they had made. Nor did he want followers that would say, 'Paul converted me', or 'Apollos baptised me.' We are all too easily influenced by human individuals and their gifts. You can see this so abundantly in the way the world idolises sportsmen and pop stars and loves to be told every detail of their lives so that they can wear what they wear, eat what they eat, imitate what they do. Their influence and power over others is huge. Where would the Church be if all her leaders and all her faithful were subjected to the same sort of scrutiny? Needless to say the Church does have her saints and these have had their part to play. The whole point of Paul's message to the Corinthians is:

> God chose what the world looks down on and despises, and thinks is nothing, in order to destroy what the world thinks is important. This means that no one can boast in God's presence. But God has brought you into union with Christ, and God has made Christ to be our wisdom (1 Cor 1:28–30).

There is another reason why it is not vital for the apostles to have been out of the ordinary. It's not that there is little to tell about them as individuals, but because it's not as individuals that their importance and influence lies. It's because they belonged to a group, a body of people that was now the nucleus of God's Kingdom, God's Church. 'The whole is greater than the sum of the parts.' We are constantly marvelling at incredible machines which defy the laws of nature and the power of our imagination. The jumbo jet that flies, the ocean liner that stays afloat, the computer with its millions of circuits, not to mention the human body. Take any of these to pieces and you have a worthless heap of junk on your hands. Put them together as a whole and they work. 'The whole is greater than the sum of its parts.' The influence of the group is greater than that of the individual.

When Jesus chose the Twelve, he was selecting his team, his squad to send into the harvest. As individuals they weren't up to much; put them together, with the power of the Holy Spirit coursing through their veins, and you have the mystery of the Church. It was together, in communion with one another and with their Lord, that their strength and influence lay.

Today, it is the growth in individualism which challenges the value and meaning of the institution, especially the Church. Why is there this massive shift away from belonging to any form of group? Is it the all-powerful effect of the individual pop star or sportsman which makes people seek individual glory and shun the far greater benefits of belonging to the institution? It's all very well naming the man of the match, the sportsman of the year – even the choirboy or choirgirl of the year. I'm not denying the place of excellence. I don't want to play down the need for the spirit of competition which drives people to pursue these ends. The inevitable upside of the publicity given them, however, is to deny any real significance or importance to the team that won the game, the choir the choirboy or girl belonged to.

All I can say in conclusion is that Jesus chose ordinary men and women and formed them into his Church because at the end of the day the Church would last and have far greater influence than any one individual in her. The jumbo jet of the Church will get you to heaven whereas a heap of jumbo parts won't get you anywhere!

More than any sparrows

12ᵗʰ Sunday, Ordinary Time (2008)

In today's gospel, Jesus tells us to 'fear no one'. This doesn't call for reckless behaviour on our part, but for commitment to the message *of* Jesus and the message *about* Jesus. 'Everyone who acknowledges me before others I will acknowledge before my heavenly Father' (Mt 10:32). Jesus is warning the apostles of their greatest enemy, worldly fear. In spite of his warning, Peter's fears did not go away. The apostles were frightened by the storm; Peter cursed and swore at the little housemaid on the night of his Master's arrest. Even after the Resurrection, the disciples were hiding behind closed doors for fear of possible arrest. It needed the Holy Spirit to enable them to overcome their fears and go and preach boldly.

The gospel is about whom we should fear and whom we should not be afraid of. The readings may be stern stuff in some ways, in other ways they are realistic in that they concern themselves quite openly with the brokenness of this world – the pain, the sinfulness, the suffering, not to mention the ruined lives of so many refugees and immigrants fleeing from terrorism in their own countries. And now, with the *fearful* price rises in the essential commodities of our lives, there can be few people who are not deeply concerned about the future. It is hard not to be afraid.

A survey tried to discover the principal sources of fear that people have today. Most were not all that surprising. Fear of dying was No. 1, fear of heights, fear of failure. The list goes on. However, there was one entry which you might not have thought about before which was at position No. 2 in the top ten list of fears – the fear of public speaking. It was high on the apostles' list before the coming of the Holy Spirit.

Fear is probably the most destructive force in our lives. What the survey did not mention was the survey before the one on what you fear most, namely what is the thing that spoils life most for you? What comes between you and happiness? Many people are unhappy simply because fear dominates their lives. Fear makes them less in control of who they are and over the events that run their life. God doesn't want us to be afraid. Love casts out fear. Yet fear, and its near relatives of worry and anxiety produce envy, lack of confidence, inferiority, feeling unwanted. So much good in peoples' lives never sees the light of day because of their fears.

Shakespeare in *Julius Caesar* states:

Cowards die many times before their deaths; the valiant never taste death but once. Of all the wonders that I have yet heard, it seems to me most strange that men should fear; seeing that death, a necessary end, will come when it will come (*Julius Caesar*, Act 2, 1.30).

We need to be examining our lives frequently to see in what areas we are being held back or bound by fear. We can be like Lazarus trapped or imprisoned in the darkness of the tomb. We need to be unbound so as to be free. Fears relate to three things: fears relating to God, fears regarding others and fears about yourself. For many fear of God is deep. Fr Gerard Hughes' book, *The God of Surprises*, still a bestseller, describes well the different attitudes and approaches people have to God. People are terribly afraid of God, afraid to love him, afraid he doesn't love them, afraid they are not doing his will. Cardinal Hume left us with a touching image of what God is like. He describes how when he died he would be able to sit on God's knee and tell him the whole story of his life, as a child would to his father. Our Christian faith helps us more than anything to overcome our fears and become more fully human, more alive. 'God calls us out of darkness into his own wonderful light.'

Fear not only warps our judgement about God, but also about ourselves and others. The gospel is directed at the very fear we have of others and not being true to ourselves and our beliefs. Fear of what others think of us cripples so many and is one reason why so many are afraid of speaking in public. It's not the bad eggs or tomatoes they are afraid of, it's simply what others are thinking of them. Fear makes us imagine the worst. We worry about how we look, how we sound, how we live, where we live. Fear makes us afraid to be ourselves. Worse, it makes us pretend, makes us try to be what we are not. I know, in all this, there are extremes that have to be avoided. Lack of respect for others and their rights leads to irresponsibility and carelessness which are as much a prevailing ailment of society as are fear and anxiety.

The third area of fear is in relationship to others. Fear makes us afraid to reach out to others. It makes us distrustful and suspicious. We project and assume all the wrong things. Rivalries and dissensions are so often prompted by fear, by imagined threats; fear that others threaten our job, our family, our position. Without Christ's example of love and how he overcame hatred by love and forgiveness, the way forward would be closed.

Into all this comes fear of the unknown future and the pointless fears we burden ourselves with about it. 'I have had many worries in my time and none of them ever happened.' Ultimately, we must keep in mind the words of the psalmist: 'When cares increase in my heart your consolation calms my soul. When I think I have lost my foothold your mercy, Lord, holds me up.' 'So there is no need to be afraid; you are worth more than hundreds of sparrows.'

Welcome

An American priest, writing about his parish, described the success with which the parish had been built up. Liturgy groups, prayer groups, social justice groups and the parish council were all working smoothly and enthusiastically. You couldn't have wished for a better parish. Even the priest was well pleased with how everything was going.

Until, one Sunday morning, when all his illusions were shattered. The previous day a group of refugees had arrived in the small town and a civic appeal was made for homes in which the refugees could be temporarily housed. Not one family in the parish offered to open their house to one of those refugees. The priest realised that his parish was little more than an empty shell. The parish was unable to share its life by extending a welcome to others.

Imagine if refugees had arrived in your parish and an appeal had gone out to people for homes. Today's Mass reminds us that we are walking in the footsteps of our Master and we will be judged by the welcome we give to others. 'Anyone who welcomes you, welcomes me.' This is no more than a further clarification of the teaching we had a couple of weeks ago: going two miles, if asked to go one; giving your jacket, if asked for a shirt.

To be always welcoming is a hard standard to achieve and maintain. It is founded on the law of love: to love your neighbour as yourself. It is also tied in to that other gospel maxim we heard today: 'Anyone who does not take up his cross and follow me is not worthy of me.' Sometimes, we are called to welcome those who are more of a cross than a pleasure. You know how we say of people, 'Oh, he's a pain!'

In fact, you might go so far as to say, what Jesus is asking today is that we welcome our crosses! Welcome the people who make you cross! People sometimes say to me: 'I'm awfully sorry to trouble you', or 'I hope I'm not being a nuisance', and I, if I know the person well enough, will say, 'Not to worry, we welcome nuisances here.' We don't mind being troubled by friends. The difficulty is when we are troubled by those we don't care for. Henri Nouwen expressed it very succinctly in his book *Reaching Out*. He called it 'from hostility to hospitality'. Often we start out hostile to people and ideas and we have to gradually bring ourselves to being hospitable to them.

Some years ago, in the church in France 'welcome' was the 'in thing'. It was the key to a positive attitude to all the changes going on at the time, as well as fulfilling a basic gospel precept. Although you can make a spirituality of welcome, it demands a high level of unselfishness and openness. Each of us has many crosses thrust upon us: but hardly any are quite so persistent or so difficult as the cross which consists of these intruders who break up our comfort and routine. We like to control our own life, plan what we'll do and when we'll do it. My life is my own; I do with it what I like. It is our most basic instinct to feel possessive and protective of our time and money.

As I know from running the guesthouse, and as you more than likely know from your own experience, interruptions and unwelcome people keep upsetting our day. It is a basic instinct to feel that our life is our own. When someone interrupts us, the temptation is to complain 'my day has been mined'. The gospel phrase, 'he who loses his life for my sake will find it' has this sort of situation in mind. It's when your day has been ruined, lost so to speak, that you are in the best position to fulfil the gospel precept.

Our life is not our own. It belongs to God. When God comes to you in a member of your family, or the unexpected visitor, you must welcome that person, realising that they have only a right to take back from you some of the life that has been given you by God. To find life, you have to lose it to others, as Jesus himself did.

How welcoming are we as individuals, as a family, as a parent, as a Church? I remember one lady telling me how she had gone to a new parish. She said she needn't have existed for the amount of attention anyone paid to her. In these times when so many are moving in or out of the area, there are bound to be newcomers to the parish. Some parishes have a register at the back of the church for newcomers to write their names in. Nevertheless, that still doesn't relieve us of the responsibility of noticing the new family and making them welcome.

Nor must we confine ourselves to people. Whenever we find ourselves resenting new ideas, changes, outsiders who threaten our old ways of thinking, we are failing in welcome. We are not recognising the Lord when he comes to us.

Mother Teresa was once asked by a group of businessmen for a word of advice. She said: 'Smile at each other.' A smile is always a sign of welcome. It used to be said of progressives: 'they never smile'. The unsmiling take themselves too seriously. It is very easy to be too busy to smile. A smile puts the other at ease. Even babies smile to put a worried mother at ease! It has been said that the message of Lourdes is one of repentance and penance. It is something much more significant than that; it is that the lady smiled.

Understanding God's presence

14th Sunday, Ordinary Time (1990)

Our monastery has just held a symposium on St Bernard whose 9th centenary it is. Those taking part had to be met at various points of arrival. I went to Heathrow to meet a monk from Belgium. Airports can be quite interesting places, seeing all the people coming and going. But they are very impersonal places. Apart from the people you are with there is scarcely any communication between all those people.

As I waited for our monk to arrive, I had plenty of time to observe the passengers as they came out of the Customs Hall – their eyes went out of focus as they tried to pick out someone they knew from all those people standing there. Then, they would spot the person who had come to meet them. Their faces lit up and they would be transformed. You could see immediately these people knew each other, they were *present* to one another in a way neither I nor anyone else there was present. It seems to me this experience can help us understand a bit better how Jesus can be present at our Sunday Mass.

Let me just carry the airport situation a bit further. I'm sure many of you, like myself, will know someone – a friend or relation – who has gone overseas to emigrate or to work (or both). *Physically*, you are no longer *present* to each other. For a person to be *really* present he or she has to be there in the flesh. But they can be present in other ways. You can write as often as possible and occasionally talk to them on the phone – *hear* their voice. You can tell them all that's going on back home, and how everyone is. So you may be separated and absent in one way, in another way you keep *in touch*. We use that very phrase. We say *Keep in touch*: Touch is something physical. A person is really present when you can touch them physically. If we can't touch them physically, we can do the next best thing and keep in touch in these other ways: writing, phoning, sending photos.

Another way of understanding how someone can be present even though not physically present here in the room with you, is to notice that the very word *present* has more than one meaning. For example, you are all *present at mass*. I am present. Jesus is present too, 'where two or three are gathered together, I am present too'.

But present also means a moment in time: the present moment. I like the story of the child who came home from school all in tears. When his mother asked him what was the matter, he explained that the teacher had told him to 'stand there for the present and she never gave me one!'

Now even if you are not present to each other by being in the same room, you can still be present to someone by being aware of all that is going on in their life – their health, their marriage, their children, their friends. This kind of knowledge and love has to be constantly updated, constantly brought up to the present if you are to keep in touch.

Let us now return to the airport for a moment and the meeting with this friend. It's not like two strangers meeting with awkward pauses and little to talk about. It's the very opposite. You are bubbling over with things you want to say, both talking at the same time. And the simple reason is because, though you may have been separated, you have kept in touch. You are present, up to the moment with each other.

The question, then, I want to put to you is this. Who at that airport is more present to you? All those people standing there waiting for someone, or your friend who is still to emerge from the Customs Hall? The first may be physically present. But the absent person is more really present because of the knowledge and love you have of them.

At Mass, that is precisely how Jesus is present: first in his word, then in his body and blood. 'Do this in memory of me.' Do it to keep alive my memory in your minds and hearts. We're here at Mass because Jesus has gone away for a while. He is absent. But we know 'he will come again'; we know we will be meeting him at the airport of heaven when we shall reach the fullness of his presence. In the meantime, we try through prayer, through hearing his word, through the sacraments to keep alive his presence in our minds and hearts. So that when he comes again we will be right up to the present, we will recognise him, like the disciples on the road to Emmaus.

Words, words, words

15th Sunday, Ordinary Time (1984)

Words, words, words! Each day an endless stream of words pours into our minds through what we hear and read. Each day our minds are bombarded by an infinite variety of words, a variety so great that it is impossible to digest them all. And yet this is the nature of our minds. They simply never stop during the day – or even during the night if you are unlucky enough not to be able to sleep. A boy once asked his dad who made the first talking machine. His father replied, 'God made the first talking machine; Edison made the first talking machine you could switch off.'

And just as our minds never stop thinking so our ears never stop hearing. While we are awake all our senses are switched on. We are hearing all the time, we are seeing all the time, we are feeling all the time, smelling all the time. However, they may be switched on all the time but our attention is not on all the time. There is, tucked away in each of us, a control room where we are sifting and filtering this endless stream of words coming into us. It is saying, 'this is interesting, that isn't. Listen to that, don't bother about that'. So our ears which are hearing the words start to listen attentively; our eyes which are seeing all the time start to look – something has caught their attention. Our noses which are smelling all the time catch a smell which starts the mind thinking of food or some memory associated with that smell.

It's something of a mystery how the little man in our control room decides what to listen to and what not, what is interesting and what is boring, what is important and what isn't. Already during this Mass we have been hearing a lot of words, but how many of us have been listening to them? How many of you can tell me what the readings were about? How many could even tell me what they have been thinking about? The little man in our control room although he has some say in what we think, has to deal with a mind that is easily distracted, easily diverted from one thing to another. It is virtually impossible to concentrate for long on one subject – as any student knows to his cost.

The gospel was about the sower and the seed. The sower is God and the seed is his word. The soil it is sown in is our hearts and minds. The different types of soil represent the life situations which could prevent the 'word' from 'bearing fruit'. How does the Word of God take root in my heart? How does it grow and bear fruit? First and foremost we must be good listeners. As I just said, there is all the difference in the world between hearing the gospel and actually listening to it. Everyone heard the gospel but not everyone listened to it with attention.

Listening to the scriptures has its problems; it's not like listening to the news which is new and interesting. This is precisely the message of today's gospel. Before ever the Word of God can bear fruit we must listen to it, receive it with open minds and hearts.

We may have heard the word, the gospel before; maybe it is sleeping in our memory. The whole point of hearing it again is to disturb the slumber, is to wake us up once more to the message of Christ in the gospel.

The word of God is powerful enough to change us if we take it to heart. It does not go back to God empty. Just imagine if we heeded only one saying of Our Lord and put it into action, for example, 'Judge not'. What a different person each of us would become. How many rash judgements would be avoided, how many unnecessary misunderstandings?

Let us then be like those who received the seed in the good soil of a generous heart. Be like Our Lady, in other words, who heard the word of God and kept it.

The wheat and the darnel

16th Sunday, Ordinary Time (2005)

The parable of the wheat and the darnel faces the very human question of when to correct and when not to correct. It's a recurrent dilemma and seemingly contradictory answers are given. Isn't this parable contrary to what Our Lord said on another occasion about, 'If your eye offend you cut it out, if your hand offend you cut it off' (Mt 5:29)? That's a more radical approach. Today the emphasis is on tolerance and leniency.

'There is so much bad in the best of us and so much good in the worst of us that it little behoves any of us to say owt about the rest of us.' This old saying would seem to be relevant in the context of today's gospel. So much bad in the best of us … We would all like to be perfect and be saints but in what does human perfection lie? It's not like the weed-free field of wheat we can see as we travel along the road. The immaculate crop, punctuated at regular intervals by the tracks where the tractor passed first with the weed-killer, then with the insecticide. A perfect crop, but there are no birds for there is no undergrowth to nest in and no insects to feed on. From a farmer's point of view, it's a perfect, darnel-free crop, but from the nature lover's point of view it's a disaster: the price is too great. Human perfection is far too complex and full of paradox to be defined as easily as that.

I remember Fr Anthony, my junior master at the time, saying to me, 'There is no such thing as a perfect monastery or community, a perfect choir or a perfect monk. The monastery that has failed is where serious faults and breaches of the rule go unchecked.' The point of the observation is that some weeds have to be pulled out whilst other weeds can and even should be left. Field Marshal Montgomery once said: 'I would have saved myself a lot of trouble had I made trouble at the start.' Abuses that are allowed to grow are much harder to eradicate if they're allowed to take root and flourish. In what sense, then, are we to understand Our Lord's advice to leave the darnel in? We read in this morning's passage from St Gregory of Palamas that one good reason for not pulling up the darnel straight away is because some people change their ways and improve with time. If they had been pulled up immediately, they would never have had that chance. Children have their faults; we don't jump on them for every childish misdemeanour.

To pull out the weeds or to 'pull out' altogether is not a clear-cut choice. Who's to decide when a weed is bad enough to pull out, or when is a community so bad that you would do the right thing to 'pull out' and leave? I say community, but the same principle applies right across the vast spectrum of human living. One need only try to think of a perfect NHS, or a perfect Government, or a perfect Church, or, closer to home, a perfect family, or a perfect parish. There's no such thing. I heard only this week of a church up north that had a sign outside which said: *The perfect church for the imperfect.* It is self-evident that the Church is not perfect and that it comprises saints and sinners. 'To live above with the saints we love that is glory. To live below with the saints we know that is another story.' Where do we draw the line between acceptance and tolerance of human imperfection and weak, irresponsible overlooking of grave misconduct? St Benedict returns to the question of discipline and correction of faults in the monastery time and again in his Rule. It would not be too farfetched to say his Rule is a commentary on this parable. He has a lot of wise advice for the abbot on the qualities of a good shepherd of the flock. He warns him that he is answerable to God for the conduct of the monks. Yet, he reminds him not to scrape away too hard at the rust or he might make a hole in the pot and do more harm than good. He is not to break the crushed reed or quench the wavering flame.

What is the parable really telling us? Everyone was asleep when the enemy came and sowed the darnel among the wheat. Is this a wake-up call? Wheat and darnel are not easy to distinguish. Maybe, the first lesson the parable is teaching us is vigilance. It means being aware of what is right and wrong, what is bad and what is good. It's a challenge. The other answer comes with the words, 'Let them both grow till the harvest.' That gives us all a second chance, a breathing space, time to pull out some of the darnel in our own lives. There's the rub, too! There's going to be a harvest. The warning is we'll have to give an account. The good news is the Lord is good and forgiving, slow to anger and rich in mercy. Somehow we have to keep growing in spite of all the darnel all around us. It means not losing sight of Jesus. Follow him and he will lead us through the darnel of this life.

To be thirsty is to be human

18th Sunday, Ordinary Time (2008)

O come to the water, all you who are thirsty.

In biblical times that would have been a fine slogan to have written above a soft drinks stall. If you had the next words – 'though you have no money, come' – on your stall, you would definitely do a brisk trade but would also soon be out of business.

The Bible often uses thirst as a symbol of our relationship with God. In hot countries like Israel, thirst is felt more, especially when fresh water is hard to come by. Hot or cold country, we all experience thirst and you see people everywhere carrying a bottle of water. In the psalms, thirst is often used as an image of spiritual longing. 'Like a parched land my soul thirsts for you' (Ps 142:6). 'Like parched land' that's the kind of language we can identify with. We feel our spiritual life is like a dried up river. 'O God, you are my God, for you I long; for you my soul is thirsting. My body pines for you like a dry, weary land without water' (Ps 62). Or again: 'Like the deer that yearns for running streams so my soul is thirsting for you, my God' (Ps 41).

In the gospels, Jesus often uses thirst as an image. 'If anyone is thirsty, let him come to me' (Jn 7:37). Notice how he invites us to come to him, to slake our thirst just as Isaiah had said: 'O come to the water, all you who are thirsty' (Isa 55:1). Jesus' conversation with the Samaritan woman by the well comes to mind. 'Whoever drinks this water will be thirsty again, but whoever drinks the water that I will give will never be thirsty again … Sir, the woman replied, give me that water: Then I will never be thirsty again' (Jn 4:13–15).

Can you see, then, Our Lord is trying to draw our attention to something important? What we are being asked to do is realise that we have spiritual thirst and that there is only one way to satisfy it and that is go to Jesus. 'Pay attention. Come to me', is what Isaiah said. Our very neediness is in itself our answer to God's invitation to come to him. How often does Jesus say 'come', 'come to me' in the gospels: 'Come to me all you who labour and are heavy burdened and I will give you rest.'

It often seems to me that our world has become so preoccupied with green issues, world poverty, peace and justice – worthwhile issues in themselves – that it has lost sight in the process of the poor individual, the likes of you and I, who hunger and thirst for God. When you are hungry or thirsty, there's an empty feeling inside, a feeling of incompleteness, of needing still more. You can get up from the table feeling hungry, you can leave the pub still feeling thirsty. But this inner craving, this inner spiritual hunger, is not just restricted to food and drink, something to fill our belly with. It applies to our whole life and the need for something to fill our lives with. We hunger for intimacy and friendship and love; we hunger for novelty, excitement, something to do, something to occupy our leisure hours with. It applies to other things: the hunger we have for beauty: jewellery for the body, beautiful objects around the house and garden.

And what happens? The answer is there in the first reading: 'Why spend money on what is not bread, your wages on what fails to satisfy'? We see a pleasure-seeking world looking for new ways of trying to satisfy their hunger and thirst, their craving for distraction. 'Do not lay up for yourselves treasures on earth ... lay up treasures in heaven ... where your heart is ...'

Don't get me wrong: I'm not suggesting that if we come to the Lord we will never thirst or hunger again in the natural sense. To be human is to be hungry and thirsty; it means you are alive. Not to have feelings and desires, not to have wants and needs is to be dead. If you haven't got any feelings inside you, you are dead. To be alive, to be unsatisfied within will be something that will be with us until the day we die.

The reason why the gospel today about the feeding of the 5,000 finds its place here is because it shows Jesus never turning people away. Jesus fed them so full that 'they all ate as much as they wanted' and there were twelve baskets over. The twelve baskets over means there is always more where Jesus is. Only Jesus can fulfil our deepest spiritual longings. 'Come to the water, then, all you who are thirsty.'

The message today is this. If we feel spiritually thirsty, like parched land, we are blessed. 'Blessed are you when you hunger and thirst, God will satisfy you': his Word that is, will give meaning and purpose to our lives. Jesus will more than satisfy us: 'Nothing can come between us and the love of Christ ... [Nothing] can ever come between us and the love of God made visible in Christ Jesus our Lord.'

'Sure Trust'

21ˢᵗ Sunday, Ordinary Time (1981)

> ... *And the gates of Hell can never hold out against it* (Mt 16:18).

> *Our faith is nothing else but a right understanding and true belief and sure trust that with regard to our essential being we are in God and God in us, though we do not see him.*
>
> Julian of Norwich

The key words in that passage are *sure trust*. In a world like ours where so much is vanishing, one of the first qualities of our life in God to suffer is our *trust*.

You can see it at work, readily enough, in our attitude to the government. Many people express distrust of the monetary policy pursued by the government. Trust is not a simple attitude, for like all Christian virtues it stands between two extremes. At one extreme, there is mistrust or distrust which is lack of trust. The other extreme is excessive trust bordering on gullibility. When we are talking about trust in people and human establishments, the ideal lies in the mean, in the middle; it's a balance between overconfidence and underconfidence. But when we are dealing with our trust in God, then, provided it is rightly understood we can never trust enough. Many hymns and psalms express this; one that comes to mind is 'Praise to the holiest in the height, and in the depth be praise, *in all his words most wonderful, most sure in all his ways.*' Most sure in all his ways. We really can't trust God enough.

Human trust is a very difficult thing to achieve. How many marriages have broken up once trust has gone out the window? How many parishes or works suffer as a result of mutual distrust? You can see it at work in the family situation between parents and teenage children. A recent survey asked teenagers what the number one problem was between them and their parents? The answer: *trust.* Parents were asked the same question and they came up with the same answer: Lack of *trust* – not sex, drugs, money, exam results, religion or even the generation gap, just simply the fundamental problem of mutual trust. Parents have to prevent their children from making mistakes that can only be made once. Teenagers have to try and trust their parents in their decisions. But if parents are over cautious and don't trust their children enough, then how can the children learn how to handle life for themselves? Sooner or later they are going to be on their own and making their own decisions, so it's very important that they be prepared for this in good time.

Nor is it only a case of insufficient trust. Trust is a positive thing, something you have to convey to the other. This sort of trust builds up confidence in a remarkable way. If I know someone trusts me, trusts my decisions, has confidence in me, it breeds confidence in me. It also breeds trustworthiness. If I know someone trusts me, then I'm anxious in the right sense not to belie that trust by acting irresponsibly.

An example of this trust at work could be seen at the royal wedding. I'm not thinking of the royal couple so much as of the crowds and the police. After the Brixton and Toxteth riots the police got a bad press. They were said to be provocative and inciting people by their harsh treatment. There was no hint or suggestion of that at the royal wedding where the crowds quite evidently were most co-operative with the police as they walked down the Mall. The police weren't having to hold them back by force, there were no scuffles or clashes. What is the difference between the two crowds? The rioters distrust the police and take every request as a provocation. The wedding crowds trusted the police. They were governed by consent not constraint.

This brings us to our trust in God and the trust God has placed in us. For most of us, the scriptures contain special messages that build up our trust. It might be Peter walking on the waters. It might equally well be the lack of trust the disciples showed when the storm blew up and Jesus was asleep in the boat. They didn't trust him enough to know no harm could come to them with Jesus at their side, so they woke him up. 'Master, don't you realise we're sinking?'

Always, the message is the same. If you lack trust, if you are mistrusting, you lose your nerve and panic. You want to grab the steering wheel from God because you are not certain 'he is most sure in all his ways'. If, however, you have that sure trust then we can be confident that the 'gates of hell will not prevail against the Church' or against anyone who entrusts himself to the Lord. 'Oh, my Jesus, I put my trust in your loving mercy.'

Hallowed be thy name

21st Sunday, Ordinary Time (1993)

We can all remember childhood jingles such as 'I'm the king of the castle, get down you dirty rascal,' and 'Sticks and stones may hurt my bones, but names don't hurt my feelings.' I used to like that one. Like most boys I was a bit sensitive to what people called me. On reflection, though, the taunt seems sheer bravado. 'Names' do hurt ones feelings; they do stick more than sticks or stones.

Names are important or our modern world wouldn't be so obsessed about what it calls 'politically correct' language. Names like 'blind', 'deaf', 'old', 'handicapped' are all on their way out, to be replaced with such euphemisms as 'visually impaired', 'hearing loss', 'chronologically gifted' (for 'old'!), and there are any number in use instead of handicapped ... but a spade is a spade, and sooner or later, people will rumble to the fact that it still comes to the same thing whatever name you call it by. This is equally true for the naming of sins. No one commits fornication these days, they 'live together'. No one steals, things just 'fall off the back of lorries': or are 'liberated'.

Although there is absurdity and nonsense in a lot of what is happening in this area, there is also a lot of good and a lot of sense in it. We are much more sensitive to words and how names do hurt peoples' feelings. I can't go into it now, but we are much more sensitive to how we use mainly male words in religion and often seem to exclude the female. We know that women are included when we say 'brothers', or 'for us men and for our salvation', but that's because we are so used to the language. We have become unaware and insensitive to just what we are saying.

It is particularly with regard to the names with which we address God that I want to draw your attention, not from the male/female aspect of the subject. Names matter. What we call someone, or something, how we name them defines to a great extent what they mean to us. A name can be hurtful (if it's spiteful), but it can also be helpful and healing. Just think of what the Holy Name of Jesus means to so many. No prayer put it so beautifully, or so poetically, as the old Prayer for England we sometimes use at Benediction: 'May his sweet name be lisped by little ones and linger on the lips of the dying.'

The power in the name of Jesus – and in that of Mary, too – is something hard to realise. Miracles have been worked, devils cast out, temptations driven away, strength and courage found to endure suffering. As Jesus said, 'Anything you ask in my name, I will give you.'

Names are important because they reveal the level of the relationship between two persons. Until you know someone's name, you don't really know them. 'What's your name?' is the first question along the road of getting to know someone.

Our gospel today tells us about that central moment in the life of Jesus and the apostles when he asks them 'Who do people say I am?' They give answers they have heard in the streets. Then, Jesus pushes them to give their own answer: 'But you, who do you say I am?' He wanted them to give him his name. They had to decide. Peter declared that he was the Christ, the Son of the living God. It is a moment of huge truth – not just for them, but for us all.

Although this episode is reported in all four gospels, it is only in this one of Matthew's that Jesus replies by naming Peter. 'You are Peter.' To us these are some of the most significant words in the gospel. It is the source of the Church's authority; its power to teach, to guide us in the truth, to forgive sins.

Today, each of us is being asked this same question by Jesus. Who do you say I am? What does the name Jesus mean to you? What is your relationship with him? Names are vital to our faith, to our personal relationship with Jesus and his heavenly Father: 'Our father who art in heaven. *Hallowed be thy name.*' If we use these words to speak to our Father in heaven, *He* will speak those words of Isaiah to us: 'I have called you by your name. You are mine.' To which I can add what Jesus said: 'Rejoice rather that your *names* are written in heaven' (Lk 10:20).

One final point. It is not just in our prayers that we must use the name Jesus. St Paul says, 'Whatever you *do*, do it in the name of the Lord Jesus.' Every time we make the sign of the cross we are doing it for that reason.

Who do you say I am?

21st Sunday, Ordinary Time (1999)

The first reading about the replacement of Shebna by Eliakim (Isa 22:15–25) is obviously intended to focus our attention on the commissioning of Peter as leader of the Church. As with so many gospels there are lots of other aspects to attract our attention. To my mind, the question of 'Who is Jesus?' is one we can never fully answer.

Jesus even had to ask his own disciples: 'Who do people say the Son of Man is?' Books keep coming out about Jesus and films too. All reckon they can tell us who Jesus was. The Archbishop of Canterbury caused consternation when he said we didn't know if Jesus had risen from the dead. He said we knew, from historical evidence, that Jesus really lived and was put to death by crucifixion. It is true the Resurrection is not something we know scientifically, because it isn't something we can prove or verify with scientific certainty – in that sense, it is accurate to say we do not know that he rose from the dead. Nevertheless, we can still speak of knowing he rose from the dead – by faith. After all, knowledge we acquire by faith, even natural faith, is still knowledge. For example, supposing I tell you there are two bells up the tower and the big one weighs two tons. You could go up and see for yourself to be sure, but as you have no reason to doubt my word, you can say you now know there are two bells up the tower. You know by faith in my telling you.

Be that as it may, the question of who Jesus is still has to be answered. It's a bit like the six blind men who were asked to say what an elephant was without being able to see it. They each go round feeling what they could. One said it felt like a wall of tough skin. Another said there was something like a rope hanging down and maybe you were meant to pull it. Another reckoned it had things like tree stumps to support it. Each is partly right and partly wrong. That is the trouble with so many books about Jesus: they are half true and half wrong.

Today's gospel is a bit like that. Some say he was John the Baptist and others Jeremiah. Having found out who others said he was, Jesus then puts the question to the apostles – to us: 'But you, who do you say I am?' One commentator thought the question should be: 'Which Jesus do you believe in?' The all-seeing Jesus of the Sacred Heart whose eyes follow you around the kitchen? The rebellious Jesus overturning the money changers' tables in the Temple? The teenage Jesus who goes missing at twelve years of age? The baby Jesus lying asleep in the hay? The refugee Jesus of Egypt? The obedient Jesus, unmarried, still at home at thirty? The rebellious Jesus who mixed with pros and cons? The criminal Jesus executed between two thieves? The Resurrected Jesus who has given us hope that there is much more to life than we realise or dare to believe? Which one is he for you? It is only when we answer some of those questions for ourselves that we can begin to know *who* Jesus is for us.

The whole question erupts again in St John's account of the man born blind (chapter 9). John writes with wry humour. The Pharisees can't take it. Some said, 'The man who did this cannot be from God, for he does not obey the Sabbath law.' Others said, 'How could a man who is a sinner perform such miracles as these?' Divided among themselves, they asked the blind man, 'You say he cured you of your blindness – well, what do you say about him?' 'He is a prophet,' the man answered.

The authorities tried to get around it by doubting if he was really blind. They go and ask his parents. The parents confirmed their son was blind but they refused to say any more. Why? 'Because the Jews had already decided that anyone who said he believed that Jesus was the Messiah would be expelled from the synagogue.' Interesting. They didn't want to believe what they knew to be true. How often is that the case with people today? They are afraid of what he might ask of them.

You will recall how the dialogue goes on. They ask him again, 'Promise before God that you will tell the truth! We know that this fellow is a sinner.' Calling Jesus a fellow. They called him a wine bibber, a glutton, a friend of publicans at other times. The blind man replied, 'I don't know if he is a sinner, but I know I now see.' My goodness, that man had a nerve; he dares to ask them, 'Maybe you, too, would like to be his disciples?' That makes the Pharisees really furious. The blind man ends by saying, 'No one has ever been cured of blindness before

... Unless this man came from God, he would not be able to do a thing.' The Pharisees then expelled him from the synagogue.

The remarkable sequel of the story, as you know, is that Jesus goes looking for the man, and when he finds him, asks him, 'Do you believe in the Son of Man?' The man answered, 'Tell me who he is, sir, so that I can believe in him.' Jesus said to him, 'You have already seen him, and he is the one who is talking to you now.'

'I believe, Lord,' the man said, and knelt down before Jesus. That's what Peter said, too, 'You are the Christ, the Son of the living God.' Jesus reminded him it wasn't his astuteness that enabled him to say that, but his father in heaven – a gift of God, in other words. Let us thank God for this tremendous gift of faith which gives us the sure knowledge of who Jesus is.

First opinion poll

21st Sunday, Ordinary Time (2002)

Someone once made the comment that this gospel was the first opinion poll. The disciples must have had to work hard at the question of 'who was Jesus'. In the early days, if you remember, they were telling each other, 'We have found the Messiah.' For a Jew, to find the Messiah and be a follower would be a real coup. Some of them were even willing to leave John the Baptist and follow Jesus. After the Resurrection, when the Jews tried to stop them preaching by having them whipped, we are told,

> As the apostles left the Council, they were happy, because God had considered them worthy to suffer disgrace for the sake of Jesus. And every day in the Temple and in people's homes they continued to teach and preach the Good News about Jesus the Messiah (Acts 5:41–42).

Today, we are very conscious of a fascination with who's the number one. Whether it is the World Cup or the Commonwealth games, we are simply propelled from one sporting event to the next trying to anticipate who will be the top, the winner, and the best. This week it was exam results that carried us along. The great niece of one of the fathers here (Fr Hilary) got five A passes at A Level and was ranked one of the five top students in the country.

Times, then, haven't changed except Jesus conducts his own opinion poll. Jesus challenges the disciples about who they really think he is. Judging from the answers, they have already discussed this question among themselves. The Jewish leaders, too, were constantly arguing among themselves about who this Jesus was. They took exception to him preaching to them: he was the son of the carpenter. Didn't they know his mother and father and what ordinary people they were?

Slowly, but surely, Peter had grown more and more sure that Jesus was who he said he was. The Son of God. If you recall the song in *Jesus*

Christ, Superstar: 'Are you who they say you are?' That is the key question, for upon it hangs our eternity. Those keys Jesus gave Peter were not the keys to this world and being a celebrity in it, but the keys to the kingdom of heaven. It's very important that Jesus is who he said he was and that the Pope is the true successor of Peter. As so often in the gospel, Jesus isn't testing Peter, testing us, so much as giving him an opportunity to express that faith and to be confirmed in it by Jesus himself, so that he can then confirm us in our belief.

Nowadays we can never get away from the pop idols of our world. Since Elvis Presley first burnt the trail, on through the Beatles, the Rolling Stones and many others, we are terribly conscious of the fact that these are the hidden shapers of our modern world. Somehow, the underlying feeling is that to be someone you have got to be a Beatle or a Rolling Stone or a Spice Girl, or a David Beckham. The question is who decides who worships at the feet of these pop idols? – and 'worship' is the right word for they are idols and it is a form of idolatry.

Who gives them their status? We hear the words, 'media-driven', and we know what that means. The media choose who and what are to be the important people and events of our world. With all these forces shaping our thinking, we are never allowed to think for ourselves; we never actually stop to look at *who* we are. If we did, we might just realise that our true identity isn't made from the material world outside ourselves, from what the papers say. Rather it is something that emerges from some other place deep within us, a place that only the One who created us could know.

In today's story from the life of Jesus, Matthew draws our attention to this question of identity. The dialogue between Jesus and Peter captures the sense that our true identity is given by God (not the media). Peter identifies Jesus as the Son of God, but then Jesus gives Peter his name with the words: 'You are Peter and on this rock I will build my Church ...'.

It is Jesus who gives Peter his identity. Peter is Jesus-driven, not media-driven. Jesus gives meaning to his life, just as he gives meaning to ours. He gives Peter his purpose and he gives us ours too. 'You are to be my witnesses'. In Christ we see who we really are. The Vatican Council said, 'Whoever follows after Christ, the perfect man, must themselves become more human.' And the Pope, whenever he addresses young people, never fails to tell them how they must look to Jesus for their identity and purpose. Jesus is the way, the truth and the life. He is the only one that can give them their true identity and true freedom.

As we hear this gospel today for the second, if not the third time, this year, we need to remember it is not just the question *who* Jesus is and that he is the key to heaven, but *who* Jesus says we are, and what our eternal destiny in him is. So then, who are you, and where are you going?

Cross and Crown

22nd Sunday, Ordinary Time (2005)

You may have heard the story about a man whom we'll call Colin who complained to the Lord about the heavy cross he had to bear and asked for it to be lightened. The Lord offered to help and took Colin into a yard where he was surprised to find it stacked full of crosses of every size and description. Jesus told him to put his cross down with the others and to find something more suitable. Colin tried many but all of them had additional snags and difficulties. He was almost around the yard and then he found one. He turned to the Lord and was about to say – when the Lord interrupted him and said, 'That's the one you came in with.' To follow Jesus means that we are ready to take up whatever cross he asks us to bear, knowing that he carried one far heavier for our sakes.

When we were young, the idea of taking up our cross daily was good advice. The daily crosses were unavoidable and the wise thing was to take them up and be as positive as you could be about them. 'Offer it up', 'Make a sacrifice of it, dear' – axioms such as those made good sense, good positive thinking.

Not any more. In today's culture we are encouraged to rebel against all suffering and trouble and, instead, exalt *self*-development and *self*-discovery. The very mention of denying self and bearing crosses seems just stupid and silly. Why should I 'accept it as a cross?' There's no merit in giving in and giving way. The very word 'accident' is going out. If an accident happens now it's got to be someone else's fault. They must be made to pay. Such an approach does little for our souls and doesn't do much for Christian forgiveness either.

One way of approaching today's text is to make more of the distinction between true and false self. The Jerusalem Bible translates it as 'renounce self' and 'follow me'. The Revised Edition has 'deny yourself'. In other words, the gospel is saying there are two selves in each of us: one true and one false. When we take up our cross to follow

Christ we are renouncing our false self and helping our true self to grow in the likeness of Christ. That makes good sense in our blame and claim society. You give up a claim which you could make and accept the cross. To even suggest 'giving up a claim' immediately makes us want to object. Doesn't it show you how deeply embedded in our minds is this prevailing attitude of blaming someone else and not accepting our crosses, our share in our salvation.

A nun was explaining the Stations of the Cross to her class. They got to the fourth Station where Jesus meets his mother. The nun explained that even though they could not talk to each other, mother and son spoke just using their eyes. The nun asked the pupils what they thought Jesus and Mary said to each other. The class gave many answers including 'This is unfair' and 'Why me?' Finally, a little girl said: 'Sister, I know what the Blessed Mother told Jesus. She said to him, "Keep going, Jesus!" Why would a mother encourage her only son on the way to crucifixion to keep on going? Because she understood the unchangeable principle of 'no cross, no crown.'

The gospel of Christ is a coin with two sides: the cross and the crown. If we try to possess one side, the glorious side, and reject the other, the suffering side, we've missed the whole point of the gospel. The same Jesus who said, 'Come to me, all you that are weary and are carrying heavy burdens, and I will give you rest' (Mt 11:28) also said,

> If any one wants to be a follower of mine, let them renounce themselves, and take up their cross and follow me. For those who want to save their life will lose it, and those who lose their life for my sake will find it (Mt 16:24–25).

Do we come to Jesus just to be freed of our burdens or do we come to him to help us take up our cross, not to get rid of it? We come to Jesus to be freed from our meaningless and futile pursuits; and, in its place, take up the cross that leads to salvation and glory.

The world offers us the *good life*; the gospel offers us the *life of goodness*. It did not all go well with Jesus; he still had to endure the cross. It did not go well with Mary; a sword of sorrow would pierce her soul. It did not and does not go well with countless men and women who keep to the gospel teaching of renouncing self to follow Christ. Why should we expect things to be easier for us?

In *theory*, we don't expect things to be easier; we accept the purpose of the cross as part of life. We don't stop competitors in the Tour de France or the London Marathon because of the pain and effort they will have to endure. If we did we'd deprive them of their crown which will make it all worthwhile. In *practice*, though, we are like Colin always on the look out for a lighter cross.

CLOSING PRAYER

Do not be conformed to this world, but be transformed by the renewing of your minds, so that you may discern what is the will of God – what is good and acceptable and perfect.

Am I my brother's keeper?

23rd Sunday, Ordinary Time (1981)

St Paul tells us in the second reading, 'Love is the one thing that cannot hurt your neighbour.' And Jesus says (in the gospel), 'If your brother does something wrong, go and have it out with him.' If he listens you win your brother back, if he doesn't listen you get two or three more to sustain the charge.

I think the obvious implication here is that the culprit is hard of heart and only needs pressure putting on him to make him come to heel. The response, 'O that today you would listen to his voice! Harden not your hearts', tends to confirm this impression.

Fraternal correction is a far more delicate business than that. In principle, yes, I am my brother's keeper; I am responsible for his spiritual and even material welfare. In practice, there are other values to maintain, other ways of winning your brother, than downright confrontation.

It's not that I'm trying to water down the gospel message and take the side of the 'wets', pussyfooting round the wrongdoers because I'm basically a funk and haven't the courage to face up to someone whom, 'more than just me' thinks is in error. The fact is, much of the evil in our world today can be attributed, traced back, to the faint-heartedness of good men who failed to speak out in time against the hard-heartedness of bad men.

And, if we do go and have it out with our brother, we'll find ourselves up against an arsenal of evasive weapons: 'mind your own business', 'interfering busy-body', 'internal affairs', 'free collective bargaining', 'let women decide their fate, not the church or state'; and that's not mentioning the small arms of defence mechanisms and rationalisation. If you can get through that lot you will have won your brother indeed.

Having the courage to do it is one thing, but having the sensitivity and compassion to confront the person when he can bear it without being hurt and crushed there you have a very different issue. Many people today are deeply wounded in parts of their personality that are beyond healing by the simple use of blunt correction. They are not ready for it and we must practise much patience, trying to support them when and how we are allowed. They are too insecure to treat with a frontal attack. 'Love is the one thing that cannot hurt your neighbour.'

Furthermore, we often expect too much too soon. People need time and space to grow, if we'll let them, especially children – and that means grow through their mistakes. In this respect, Jesus' example is interesting. He is merciless with the pharisees, but with sinners and humble folk hardly a word of criticism, even the Samaritan woman with five husbands. The Lord doesn't tell us to correct seventy times seven but to forgive. 'Love is the one thing that cannot hurt your neighbour.'

Forgiveness and memory

24rd Sunday, Ordinary Time (1999)

Forgiveness is like playing golf, driving a car, making brown bread; it sounds straightforward and simple in theory. Putting it into practice is a very different matter. We can read how important it is, we can listen to our Lord telling Peter he has got to forgive seventy times seven, we know how destructive not forgiving can be. Nevertheless, we still balk when it comes to letting go of resentment and grudges. Scripture reminds us 'not to harbour grudges', 'not to let the sun go down on your anger', 'do not seek revenge', 'be reconciled with one another'.

Forgiveness is certainly love's toughest task, and love's hardest part. Life cannot go on without the daily necessity to forgive someone something. When we pause at bedtime to say sorry to God for our offences, we also need to ask ourselves whether we have forgiven those who have offended us, even if it's only the traffic warden for giving us a parking fine. All those irritations that come our way each day usually entail an internal act of forgiveness, if it's not going to turn sour and become something that wrankles and festers.

As children, we all enjoyed the delicious irony of seeing the villain in cartoons caught out by his own weapon. Tom and Jerry are full of such misadventures. Or the canon going off just as Sylvester pokes his head down the barrel trying to unblock it, or the boomerang unfailingly returning to almost knock the head off the thrower.

Today's parable is from the same stable of stories. Forgiveness is a fast-returning boomerang. If you want to be forgiven your debts, you cannot the next minute go demanding money from a servant in debt to you.

The need for forgiveness in our world today was never more fundamental. All the world over, countries are split and divided by some conflict from the past. It doesn't require much imagination to know how well-nigh impossible it must be for one side to forgive and forget what the other side has done to it.

Yet, the paradox of the parable is that those who remember forgive. It wasn't a case of the servant remembering the debt his fellow servant owed him. It was not forgetting what his master had forgiven him that is crucial. We'll never forgive if we recall an injury. We'll only succeed in forgiving by remembering the times the Lord or others have forgiven us the hurtful things we have done. We tend to remember every slight and hurtful thing done to us and forget all the very many times when I, myself, experienced the gracious compassion of a tender loving God.

It is a sobering thought that the marks of Jesus' wounds remained after the Resurrection. Why did he still have the marks in his risen body when in all other respects it was an entirely new body? He retains the marks of the wounds, not to remind him of the terrible things we have done to him. 'See what they did to me! Can I ever forgive or forget what they did in return for all I did for them?' No, he kept the marks of the wounds lest we forget how much our sins have cost him and what enormous debts he has forgiven us. However frightful the things others have done to you or me, it can't be as bad as what the least of our sins have done to Jesus.

It is then, the memory, not of the injuries, but of the times we have been forgiven that enables us to forgive others. Forgiveness is the hallmark of a true follower of Christ.

Today's message is clear and stark. The person who cannot forgive others breaks down the very bridge over which he or she must pass one day. If you have long since given up the idea of entering heaven through the door marked 'Canonised Saint', or 'Martyr', the good news is that you and I will find the key to the back door under the mat is marked 'Forgiveness'.

The false description

26th Sunday, Ordinary Time (1978)

Does anyone love his neighbour anymore? Sorry if I sound a bit soft-boiled this morning, but this attack was brought on by the helpless feeling I get every time the country's industrial equilibrium gets upset. So often the demands seem unreasonable and unjustified. They have no thought for the suffering and financial hardship their industrial action may have on others. I can safely mention the French air controllers' dispute because it happened abroad. Yet its effects were felt very definitely in this country and at a time when they hurt most. And what did it have to do with us? At the risk of offending one of you who is in sympathy with any particular dispute – be it the firemen, the teachers, the hospital workers or the car workers – we do have to ask ourselves (as a nation and as a Church) have I no other neighbour than my fellow union member? Does it make any difference if my wage-claim might put someone else out of his job, send inflation soaring again, and more important still, perhaps, make the lot of the third world that much worse?

Reading what St Paul was saying to the Philippians today brought on this rash of bad thoughts, or bout of rash thoughts, about my neighbour in the unions. But when you read it, it does make you pause and think a bit.

If our life in Christ means anything to you, if love can persuade at all, or the spirit that we have in common, or any tenderness and sympathy, then be united in your convictions and united in your love, with a common purpose and a common mind. There must be no competition among you, no conceit; but everybody is to be self-effacing. Always consider the other person to be better than yourself, so that nobody thinks of his own interests first but everybody thinks of other people's interests instead.

If we all had that mind, the mind that was in Christ Jesus, then wouldn't the world be a different place? How right G. K. Chesterton was when he said: 'It's not a case of Christianity having been tried and found wanting. It's been tried and found too difficult.' And now it's not even tried. It's too inconvenient, too demanding – to put the interests of others before my own, to own less and share more.

The story is told of a famous Catholic Evidence speaker. A haggler, a very dirty and unkempt figure, objected that religion had existed for 2,000 years and what good had it done for the world. He mentioned some of the troubles that are still present. The speaker replied: 'Water, too, has been around for two thousand years and what good has it done for you?'

I know, basically, what we are up against is unredeemed human nature, with the greed, pride, selfishness, laziness, etc. that goes with it. That is why people put their own self-interest first and second, the greater good of the greater number which is what the Government tries to put first. However, no one likes to admit this basic selfishness and so they look round for a nice formula to wrap it up in and so convince us all that their demands were, after all, perfectly reasonable and no one should be jealous or envious.

How to distinguish the just from the unjust wage-claim is not easy – and it's not my job. What I want to do – and it is my job and yours – is to learn the clever and devious ways we are influenced and persuaded to back this group, buy this article, sympathise with this cause.

Every housewife knows the Trade Descriptions Act. If she buys something from what it had on the label and finds that it falsely described what was inside she is entitled to her money back. This act is doing us a tremendous service. I only wish that we had a thousand more laws like it to prevent other equal injustices. We meekly 'buy' lots of other kinds of goods because as they are described they sound all right.

For instance, certain countries often defend injustices going on by labeling them 'internal affairs'. Once a national flag has been hoisted over some flagrant abuse or a civil right nobody is allowed to say anything or interfere. I would venture to suggest the Unions in this country are trying a similar dodge by claiming this right to free and normal collective bargaining. It makes it sound as if the government had no right to interfere or had no authority in this 'internal affair' to lay down a pay policy.

Abortion and euthanasia are two other old favourites that come in for this type of false description. 'Not the Church, not the state, let the women decide their fate' – so the slogan goes. With a bit of window-dressing and a few misleading slogans and we go away thinking 'what's wrong' or 'why not'. The Church, however, isn't fooled. Wrap the foetus up how you will, call it what you will, it is still a human being, it still has a right to life.

A final case, although one could go on indefinitely, is 'keep politics out of the pulpit'. Once again, the flag of immunity has been stuck in a certain area of activity and human behaviour which supposedly prevents the church offering any guidelines. I agree, you have to be extremely careful. There are areas where the Church or the priest cannot interfere. He has no right to encourage people to vote for one particular party. That is an individual's private affair. But there are moral rights and wrongs that the church must speak out about or fail in her duty. If that's one extreme, the other extreme is to say 'oh, leave religion out of it'. I heard of a priest who went to visit a sick parishioner. The wife met him at the door and said, 'It's very kind of you to come, Father, but please don't talk to my husband about religion, he's depressed enough already.' Since when was religion supposed to be a depressing affair? Do you see how for her religion was in the wrong wrapping? The label of religion for her was something bad, and that, surely, is a false description if ever there was one. Religion is not unpleasant, correctly understood it could have helped her husband to feel better.

I would sum up what I've been saying in this way. In that passage I gave from St Paul we have the ideal. But, as our society grows less and less Christian, people are seeking new and empty formulas that sound right to cover up their greed and selfishness. My plea is that we take extra care not to be deceived by the wrapping, still more not to wrap up our own dishonest and deceitful behaviour hoping to cover up our own neglect and lack of love of my neighbour. God is not deceived.

It's not fair

26ᵗʰ Sunday, Ordinary Time (1972)

L ast week we were listening to the parable of the vineyard owner and the workers he hired. The Church must be anxious for us to ponder this subject a little more, for in the first reading we heard: 'You object, what the Lord does is unjust.' This is what the workers complained about; and it's the same unequal distribution of life's goods that we object to. The judgements of God's justice, as they are called in Scripture, are a big mystery to us. Hardly a day goes by without some fresh experience of it: the mother of a young family dying of cancer; a child killed in a road accident, or born blind; a man with an outstanding record of service being made redundant.

You may have noticed how even young children are conscious about the fairness of the treatment they get. Parents have to be most careful about fairshares in order to keep the peace: 'One for you, one for you and one for you.' Or, 'It's Jimmy's turn this time, it was yours last time.' One knows full well that it is not entirely due to a child's sense of justice, it is more likely to be jealousy or envy at work. When parents try to be fair it is more to prevent the sulks of jealousy than to encourage justice.

Now this is where one has to tread quite carefully. If parents always insist on strict fairness the children will tend to grow up thinking that life will always follow the same pattern; and not only life, but people, bosses, governments will all extend to them unfailing fairness. As we have seen, life is not fair. We do then need to examine ourselves, either as parents bringing up children, or as grown-ups who have already received this kind of upbringing. Am I easily upset and prone to saying 'it's not fair' when others do better than I do, or, even – and this may sound surprising – am I miserable when others don't seem to be as well off as I am?

We mustn't move too fast. If possible we must keep to the middle of the road. I certainly don't mean to recommend we be downright unfair, or worse still, unjust. A child has got to learn to share things with others. Children are born selfish and parents have to train them to think of others, to share with others, to take chores in turn. And the principal way of teaching this lesson is by being fair.

There is another danger that has to be avoided and this is favouritism and partialities. It applies to all who have charge of others. Parents and teachers soon find out how easy it is to prefer one child to another and they have to steel themselves against unfairness, trying to treat each one according to his merits. I suppose most of us can look back on life and think of examples where we felt we or others were treated unfairly. One must ask though, was the treatment unfair or was it that I expected everyone to be treated the same with no regard made for differences in personal gifts and merit. The great mystery of it all is, God has his favourites. Our Lady is addressed by the Angel Gabriel as 'the favoured one of God'. The saints are saints because God loved them more and gave them more graces. The only answer one can offer is the answer God himself gives in Scripture. He likens himself to a potter and asks: 'Does the pot say to the potter "why have you made me thus and not such and such?"'

This is why I say you can take fairness with children too far and overdo it. Life does not hand out its goods evenly. Life is not fair. The man born in a refugee camp is not as well off as a man born in England. Besides differences of environment, there are the widely different amounts of talents people are born with. There are not many athletes with physical powers that will enable them to reach the Olympics. As you know, Our Lord often referred to the number of talents men receive and it was always with respect to their inequality. God will not judge us for having fewer talents than our brother, but because we have not made sufficient use of the talent or talents we have got.

Sooner or later in life, the lesson will come home to us that God's Providence does not treat all alike and there is no reason why he should. Life would be unbearable if everyone were identical. It is because not all are alike that children should be taught and grown-ups have to learn again and again not to be surprised when others seem to get on and I seem to be at a standstill.

When you consider how much of the unhappiness in our modern society stems from this simple fact, you begin to give it more serious attention. All the time it's *equality* people are shouting for: equal work, equal pay; or the coalminers are complaining because the car workers receive more. 'It's not fair!' That's what the vineyard workers mumbled when the last comers got the same as they did. 'Why be envious because I am generous?' asks the owner. And we must ask ourselves: 'Is my eye evil because my Master is generous?', because my neighbour has had success and I haven't?'

If then, in life, the goods are distributed very unevenly, one has to be most careful how one introduces a child to such a situation. Either way there are dangers. But if you do so at the cost of the child learning that even in an ideal country wealth and civil rights are not perfectly distributed, the child is going to be unbalanced. And that child may be myself, grown-up now and infected with this attitude. On the other hand, you can argue from the unfairness of life that there is no room for justice, no reason to disguise personal preferences, no purpose in striving for a more equitable solution. That too is false.

To wind up these few thoughts, let me say first of all, we are confronted with a mystery: God has not willed to give each man exactly the same. Fairshares, then, cannot be a hard and fast rule. Nevertheless, each man does have the same basic rights to life and so forth, and there must be no unfairness about these. Fundamentally, I think it comes down to seeing whether I am acting from justice and a desire to give each one his due according to his degree of merit, or whether I am acting out of jealousy and envy and trying to deprive another of his good name and his hard earned possessions.

Let me finish off with what St Paul was urging in the second reading:

There must be no competition among you, no conceit; but everybody is to be self-effacing. Always consider the other person to be better than yourself, so that nobody thinks of his own interests first but everybody thinks of other people's interests instead. In your minds you must be the same as Christ Jesus.

Two Sons

26th Sunday, Ordinary Time (1984)

A man had two sons ...

To be perfectly honest, I'm not sure which son I would identify myself with. Which one do you reckon you are like? Can I put it like this, which one would you get on with? In the lives of most people there is normally one person you have difficulty in getting on with – what psychologists call the significant other. This other person may live at home with you, he may be a parishioner, someone at the office, you may come up against him in your leisure. It may be a parent or a superior, it may be a child or a subject. You can get on with the ninety nine others but this one person comes between you and happiness. Try what remedies you like, you may get angry, you can try to be reasonable, but will you ever succeed in convincing this person of the error of his ways? He may say, 'I don't know what you're talking about, my friends don't seem to find this the case.' Or else, he may (which is worse) quite agree and promise to turn over a new leaf. Having said that, twenty-four hours later he will be exactly the same as ever. Every attempt to cure his laziness, jealousy, bad moods, touchiness or peculiar mannerisms all become shipwrecked on some basic flaw, some incurable blind spot in his character.

Here then is the first son, the one you find it difficult to get on with. What about the other son? Is he easier to get on with? I don't know. The strange thing is, he's very like his brother, except for the fact that you never see him. I mean, of course, yourself, you are the other son: there are only two sons. You too have that same fatal flaw in your character, that same incurable blind spot. All those hopes and plans of yours that were frustrated because of the first son, your brother also has, and his are being shipwrecked because of you.

You may admit – who doesn't – 'I know I have my faults', but do you realise there is also that same basic flaw in you that you can see so clearly in him, the same something which gives others just that same feeling of despair which their flaws give you? You may even say, 'But why don't others tell me? I'm only human.' And yet how many times have you been told, or have even told yourself you must do something about this or that in your character and behaviour, and are still doing it – or not doing it?

Because both these sons of God are in many respects very alike, God doesn't love one less than the other. Today's parable is intended to show that one of these sons loves God more than the other. The message is the same for both sons. For the first son, he must try and ration the amount he allows the 'significant other' in his life to dominate his thoughts. He must shove these illusions away, for he's not going to achieve a miraculous transformation overnight. Those improvements we dream about in others are going to take a long time.

As for the other son – that's you and me – be sure there is something in you that unless it is altered is going to come between you and God and deprive you of the happiness he intends for you. You may be secretly flattering yourself on having said 'yes' and gloating over the son who said 'no', and like the son who said 'yes' not done anything about it yet.

> I tell you solemnly, tax collectors and prostitutes are making their way into the kingdom of God before you. For John came to you, a pattern of true righteousness, but you did not believe him, and yet the tax collectors and prostitutes did. Even after seeing that, you refused to think better of it and believe in him.

Almighty Disappointment

27ᵗʰ Sunday, Ordinary Time (1978)

Having heard the readings about the Lord and his vineyard and all that he had done for it, how do you think he felt? How would you feel? Hurt? Angry? Cheated? Perhaps all of them because they all describe the way we feel when life doesn't deliver the goods. Yet, there is another feeling that describes more precisely still what we would feel: disappointment. If that is how God felt then it must have been an almighty disappointment!

As you know, of course, we cannot speak of God being disappointed in the way we are. Disappointment is a human feeling, like anger or resentment. It is only a manner of speaking when we refer to God as being disappointed. The message addressed to us. Remember the time when Our Lord said to his disciples 'How often would I have gathered you around me as a hen gathers her chicks and you would not' (Mt 23:37). Rejection, lack of appreciation for all God had done for Israel must have hurt God in some way, must have disappointed him somehow even if not in exactly the same way as we experience it. Yet, if we know how bad we feel in such circumstances, then we can know how others feel. Consequently, we should not, knowingly, cause someone else, especially God, to suffer because of our lack of appreciation and gratitude.

Whether we like it or not, disappointment is part of the warp and woof of life. Even children are not spared it. A young girl writes: 'When I arrived at my new school I came hoping to find friends and a friendly atmosphere. But I was soon disappointed, for I came up against cliques and I didn't feel accepted. I wanted to get on but so many of the others didn't seem the least bit interested. It was all very discouraging.'

And a boy who was attending a school run by religious tells how disappointed he was when he discovered that his teachers, whom he regarded as representing God, were far from being what he had expected. He simply could not understand this discrepancy. As a result he lost all faith in God as well as in his teachers.

I'm sure each of you would have no difficulty in giving an example from your own life were I to go around the congregation. For one it would be 'I was hoping he/she was going to be such a wonderful person to live with, but I was very disappointed.' 'I was so looking forward to our family holiday but it was terribly disappointing.' 'I was hoping for great things after the Council but it has all been a bit of a disappointment.' Yes, how many drift away from practising their faith for no other reason than disappointment? Great expectations and look ...!

Is the world, is life, one almighty disappointment? Why is it, parents and teachers, children and students, wives and husbands, businesses etc., start out with the best of intentions to make a success of it and give of their best, only to end up feeling unappreciated and terribly disappointed?

Have you noticed the sort of phrases that we have been using and use in this connection: You are disappointing. You have disappointed me. I am disappointed with you, with myself, with life. We seem to have come out in a rash of I's and you's. *I's* right, *you's* wrong. The most important thing to realise about the feeling of disappointment, as indeed is the case with all our feelings (anger, hatred, sorrow, fear, etc.), the feeling is in *me*. Yet, although it is in me, we are convinced that the cause of it is outside in someone or something else. Hence, I overlook the fact that it is my feeling and it is having an effect on me. It is rather like when we catch a cold. I will say to you 'I've caught your cold.' I'm all annoyed with you for giving it to me. But it is of little consequence where I caught it from, the fact is it is my nose, my throat, my chest that has the cold and I must do something about it.

Again, if I find Mass boring and uninteresting, that is my problem not the fault of the Mass. If you knew you were going to die today and this was to be your last Mass, I don't think it would be quite so boring.

We can go wrong in another way. If you build up an image or an ideal of a partner, a child, a church, a parent, and they don't come up to your expectations – as indeed they are hardly likely to – you become disappointed. My disappointment has come about because the standard, the ideal I had set for the other didn't correspond with that person as they *really* are. I've allowed myself to be disappointed. When you look at someone or something through a screen like this you are bound to end up feeling let down. The screen prevents you from seeing the person as he really is. It's like a camera viewfinder. You've got to get the two images to coincide in order to be in focus. If you are in focus, the picture is sure to be good.

I'm not supposing for a moment that none of us is ever going to be disappointed again. All I wanted to do today is to give some suggestions on how to handle our feelings. Besides, it is still possible for us to be genuinely disappointed, like Our Lord was. If you have done all in your power for someone and they coolly and calculatingly reject what you've done, then the other person is really to blame. To have experienced disappointment is always worthwhile. It will help us to appreciate more what others do for us and be more grateful. It will make us try harder not to be a source of disappointment to others unnecessarily. Our Lord said 'woe to the man by whom scandals come'. We can also say disappointments must come but woe to the person by whom they come, if it was deliberate.

'Sour Grapes'
– The mystery of Divine expectations

27ᵗʰ Sunday, Ordinary Time (1999)

And now inhabitants of Jerusalem and men of Judah, I ask you to judge between my vineyard and me. What could I have done for my vineyard that I have not done? I expected it to yield grapes. Why did it yield sour grapes instead? (Isa 5:3–4)

Sour grapes: it never occurred to me until now that this can be understood as a figure of speech. 'Sour grapes' is a saying used to disparage something because it is beyond one's reach. It came originally from Aesop's fable about the fox that vainly tried to get some grapes which were too far up. Finding he couldn't reach them he went away, consoling himself with the thought, 'Well, they're probably sour, so what's the point?'

The two readings about vineyards appear to have very little in common apart from the fact that they are both about vineyards. On the one hand, there is the world as creation. This vineyard is a world on which God has lavished every kind of goodness and beauty. A veritable paradise, fascinating for us to live in. God made us with needs that have to be satisfied in this world, and he provided the kind of creation that would satisfy them. His vineyard is prospering so well that men and women of our time have said, 'Thank you very much. We don't need you God; all we need is provided for in this life.' The very things God has created for our happiness have become obstacles instead of stepping stones to union with him.

On the other hand, the same can be said of the vineyard of the Church, the Lord's own creation. It has proved a lasting success – it's been around for 2,000 years – but, sadly, it has somehow lost its appeal to society in the West. It's as G. K. Chesterton so wisely put it: 'It's not that Christianity has been tried and found wanting; it's been tried and found too difficult.' Could it be said that this is a case of 'sour grapes' – 'too high, beyond our reach'? (Ps 138:6) It is unquestionably true that many find what the church asks is too much or too difficult. It does expect sacrifices – the celibacy of the clergy, the indissolubility of marriage, religious vows for life. The Lord expects our all, all that we have and all that we are for the sake of the kingdom. Are we to conclude that such divine expectations are too much for ordinary, earthbound mortals?

Many people, asking themselves such questions, wonder if Christianity isn't so sublime, so idealistic, so far beyond the reach of most normal people, as to be an unrealistic expectation – except perhaps as a now acceptable, because inevitable, form of hypocrisy or compromise.

Hypocrisy, that's just the type of thing nobody wants to be associated with, and consequently it is seized upon as a good way of belittling churchgoers. 'Well, you see, they are all hypocrites.' To which John Powell wants to reply, 'No need to worry. There's always room for one more.' Nevertheless, there remains an underlying point that we all feel to some extent. There is a gap between our ideals and our practice. Promises unfulfilled, economies with the truth, inconsistencies, and a lot of unfinished tasks. None of us is anything like what we should be. Rightly can it be argued, 'If a thing is worth doing, it is worth doing well'? If you can only be an average Christian you shouldn't, according to that, be a Christian at all. A sort of 'sour grapes'. Yet, Chesterton restores the balance by reminding us that, 'If a thing is worth doing, it is worth doing badly.' St Paul agrees: 'Where sin abounds grace does more abound' (Rom 5:20). The weak and imperfect are the very people Jesus came to heal, not the perfect and above reproach.

The real evil of 'sour grapes', something beyond our reach, is much deeper and subtler than that, however. The stakes are high. The demands of Christianity are not just the rules and regulations for admission to an elite club where it is not the end of the world if you can't get in. 'Well, they're all snobs in it. Who wants to belong to such a club?' If you don't get into Christianity, then it may matter more than you are prepared to admit. It will be a life – eternal life – or death issue, in the final count.

For many, the response to the Church and her teachings is – even if unspoken – one of 'sour grapes'. 'Sour grapes' surfaces in two familiar forms: shallowness and cynicism. Shallowness is surprisingly resourceful, and cynicism loves its certainty. Both are extremely detrimental to the church. Where shallowness and cynicism reign nothing is taken seriously, nothing ultimately matters. Anything goes. Keeping things superficial simplifies life. It shortens life's journey to a car ride to the pub, the shops, and the takeaway. Rubbishing anything serious keeps it at a safe distance from the cynic. If only people stuck to sightseeing and holidays on the 'costa-a-lot', it would be so much simpler for all! Shallowness and cynicism are modern man's answer to the serious questions life and death keep pushing up. That is how the tenants of the vineyard destroy first the representatives, namely the Church, then the Son of God himself.

Jesus' life and teaching draw us below the superficial, the shallows of this life, beyond the immediate. They beckon us to undreamed of realities. They give us hope that there is more to life and death than splashing around in the shallows.

Far from being 'sour grapes', Jesus offers us the fruit of the vine, which we will drink in the kingdom of heaven. His divine expectations are not *beyond our reach*. On the contrary, he came from heaven to bring heavenly realities *within our reach*. There is a paradox here, there has to be. The ultimate secret of our faith is that it consists not in what we have done for the vineyard, but what God has done: 'What more could I have done for my vineyard?' Heaven will be ours, not because of what *we* have done for God, but what *God* has done for us. The grapes are sour only if we think salvation comes through our own petty efforts and not from 'Christ, who calls us out of *nothing* into his own wonderful light.'

The focal point

30th Sunday, Ordinary Time (1972)

What's the difference between a rush-hour crowd and a football crowd? Why is one so disunited and the other so united? In the rush-hour crowd each person is going his own way; he is trying to get home and away from the rest as quickly as he can. Other people, if anything, are a hindrance to him, and are more likely to be a source of annoyance than of comfort. With the football crowd the boot is on the other foot, you might say, at least for the duration of the game. They all think together, they all cheer together and all groan together. Their heads all follow the ball in one united movement. The bigger the crowd the better. A few lone supporters would be a great disappointment. It really is extraordinary how so many thousands of people can act together.

What then, is the difference? The difference is that a rush-hour crowd has no centre of unity, no focal point of interest to keep their attention. The football crowd has one object in mind: the success of their team. They are absorbed in the fortunes of the game – not only at the time but for some time after. I give football as an example, but there are others. The focal point can be anything arresting – a parade, a celebrity, a joyful Christmas season. All these have the power to gain people's attention and hold it. Such occasions confer a mutual delight and fellow-feeling which one rarely experiences in a rush-hour crowd.

How does this connect up with the feast of the forty martyrs we are celebrating today. The point is fairly obvious. The Mass was the focal point of our Catholic forebears. It was the Mass that brought them together and kept them together in the face of bitter persecution. It was for saying Mass or attending it that so many of them were arrested and executed.

Times and externals may have changed, yet there can be no doubt that the Mass still holds pride of place in our life. The Mass is the one thing that still keeps us together. The presence of Jesus on our altar draws us closer to himself and closer to one another. This finds expression in Canon II: 'May all of us who share in the Body and Blood of Christ be brought together in unity by the Holy Spirit.'

The Mass is the great, uniting focal point in our lives. We saw last time how this Mass unites us with Christ's action as it was, as it is, and as it will be. Christ is the focal point. His action binds us together into 'one body, one spirit (in Christ)'. And in uniting us to himself he unites us to one another, even to those countless number of Christians who have gone before us with the sign of faith. They are 'the cloud of witnesses watching us from above' that we heard about in the second reading. As we will be saying presently, 'In union with the whole Church, with Mary, the apostles, the martyrs' and especially our own martyrs. We are united too with the Church throughout the world. We are united even with those not yet born. The Mass is like the baton in a relay race. The baton must go on; should one runner, however, be missing or fail it won't be passed on. The future relies on us to hand on the Mass, in the same way as we depended on our martyrs / forebears. Without their fidelity we would have lost the focal point of our life, the thing that gives unity to all the bits and pieces.

In the example of the football crowd, you notice how it cheers, groans and experiences all that the team goes through. In a similar way we do the same at Mass. We begin *by repenting together* of our sins and all that weighs us down; we are aroused to this as we consider how Jesus endured the shame and the suffering of the Cross on account of our sins. We are cast down by the repeated number of times we have lost to the devil. Next *we listen together* to the words of the Lord, seeking comfort and light amidst the darkness and trials of this life. Finally, *we share a meal together*, a meal with Jesus present.

The meal part begins at the Offertory when the gifts are brought to the altar. The little host is symbolic of our whole life. It is as if you were to place the keys of a car or a house on the plate to signify your wish to give these to God. You can't very well bring the car into Church. Similarly with ourselves, the host is the key signifying my whole life. These gifts are now consecrated to the Lord. They become his – they become Him. I find it always most consoling to entrust myself, my friends, my work, to the Lord; he can take so much better care of them than I can with all my worrying and anxiety. Then, after pausing to remind ourselves of all those who are present in spirit with us, we come to the moment where there takes place the exchange of gifts. In return for the 'widow's mite' we have offered, the Lord offers himself in Holy Communion. As the very word, communion, implies we are united with Jesus himself, Body and Blood, soul and divinity.

The example of the football crowd serves to illustrate how a focal point can unite a very diverse crowd of people. However, like all examples, it limps. The identification of the crowd with the players and the game is only from the touchline – or at least it should be! With us and what goes on at the Mass we are far more than touchline spectators. Heaven forbid anyone should think he is only a spectator at Mass. We are sharing intimately in all that goes on. The Mass is indeed the gripping focal point that unites us. It is also so much more for our lives and our very selves become bound up and united with Jesus and the events and actions of his life. 'I live, now no longer *I* but Christ lives in me.'

Let me end by repeating the prayer we have just used for it does 'collect' in one sentence these aspirations: 'In answer to the prayers of our martyrs grant that your people may remain firmly united in the same bond of faith and love in Christ Jesus, Our Lord.'

Jesus: The source of life

32nd Sunday, Ordinary Time (1981)

Everyone loves a wedding; and the bridesmaids have an important share in it. Having *ten* bridesmaids means it must have been a big wedding. But there's a hitch, a delay. And five of the bridesmaids find their lamps are burning low. It's a bit like running out of petrol on the motorway. It was further than you thought, and there was less petrol in the tank than you'd realised. There you are: stuck on the hard shoulder, cars passing by, and you with no petrol. 'Five of them were foolish and five of them were sensible.' Feeling foolish is just about how we would feel if we were that driver without petrol.

Talking of oil reminds me of the American space shuttle that had to be postponed because of contaminated lubricating oil. It seems oil is just as vital to getting into the heavens as it was in our Lord's parable for getting to the wedding feast of heaven. In fact, it is interesting to give the space programme a thought for a moment. To put a man into space, or land him on the Moon, there is something vital that must be done if he is to survive. The conditions of his earthly environment must be simulated as closely as possible. To climb a high mountain, or fly at a high altitude, a man needs an oxygen apparatus. To fly in outer space requires special spacecrafts and spacesuits. Someone who's been to Space Centre Houston told me the spacesuits are much larger than you'd think from seeing them on television. It's a very cumbersome affair and life wouldn't be much fun if you had to live in one permanently. But without one, a man would only be able to survive for about a minute.

As I see the parable we've just heard, there are two points to consider. It's not that a man will not be able to survive in heaven without a spacesuit, but that he won't survive – spiritually – on earth without a spacesuit of faith. This is because the world with its materialism and carnal pursuits is an extremely hostile environment to our life of faith. Granted a man might survive a bit longer than a minute without Jesus' spacesuit. The trouble is the bridegroom is delayed and just when he does turn up, it's too late. You are not ready, not prepared. You are 'dead' spiritually.

The other point is this. In the second reading St Paul tells us, 'Those who have died in Christ will be the first to rise.' The words 'in Christ' – or 'in him', or 'in the Lord' occur 164 times in St Paul's writings. The spacesuit is something you put on outside. It's an artificial shell to simulate earth's conditions. 'To put on Christ' is to be transformed from within. To be 'in Christ' means our whole nature is so transformed from within that we can, as it were, live in outer space without a spacesuit at all. For that reason, the image of oil – something inside giving light outside – is in some respects a better image than the spacesuit.

This came home to me in a new way recently. It happened in Alaska at the beginning of this century. The Indians used to light their houses with a fire burning in the centre of the room. Then the gold miners arrived. They used candles, the first movable lights seen by the Indians. Eventually, electric light came to Juneau, the capital of Alaska. One day an Indian came to town from way out in the backwoods. As he entered the town store, the storekeeper pulled the cord and a brilliant light flooded the room. This was the first time the old Indian had seen an electric light.

Next morning, he got his wife to give him some more money without telling her what for. Then he went back to the store and asked 'Nika iskum?' – 'Can I get it?' – pointing to the electric light. 'Sure' said the storekeeper, not realising where the man came from and thinking he knew all about electricity. He measured off a length of flex and fitted a socket, inserted a bulb and gave the man the parcel. Off he went. When he arrived back home, he fixed it to the roof pole of his camp house and then waited for evening, or should I say, hardly able to wait till he could give his family a big surprise. The great moment arrived. He went over, pulled the cord as he had seen the storekeeper do. It's not hard to imagine his disappointment. He had done it all exactly as he had seen the storekeeper do – *externally*, that is – but there was no light because there was no electricity.

Without Christ, we will be like the old Indian's light without electricity. With him, with this new type of current coursing through our veins we will be able to live in heaven with Jesus, and with no cumbersome spacesuit to do so. Let us, then, during this Mass, connect ourselves up to Jesus, the 'power plug' of eternal life. 'Without me you can do nothing.' 'I live now, not I, but Christ lives in me' (Gal 2:20).

The principle of indirection

32nd Sunday, Ordinary Time (1975)

Last week I was discussing the possibility of self-forgetfulness being one of the principal lessons we may have to learn in Purgatory – that is, if we have not learnt it here below. As it is one of those things which, to my mind, matters quite a lot in the Christian life, I would like to add a few more thoughts on the subject today.

In *The Screwtape Letters* (C. S. Lewis), the senior devil expresses great concern about the patient's progress in virtue and the failure of the subordinate devil, Wormwood, to do anything about it. He writes: 'I see only one thing to do at the moment. Your patient has become humble; have you drawn his attention to the fact? All virtues are less formidable to us, once the man is *aware* that he has them. Catch him at the moment when he is really poor in spirit and smuggle into his mind the gratifying reflection, 'By jove! I'm being humble …' Having all had such thoughts we know well the disruptive effect it can have. Is it better to be proud and humble about it, or humble and proud about it? Either way, the fact is, or rather the fault is being too self-conscious about it. You can't *put on* humility consciously. Humility which is put on – the hunched figure of Uriah Heap (a fictional character created by Charles Dickens in his novel *David Copperfield*) rubbing his hands, comes to mind – that's not humility at all. Humility, like nearly every other virtue, turns attention away from self. The more you think about trying to be humble the more you are concentrating on yourself. Humility could almost be defined as self-forgetfulness.

And yet, how many people you ask think of it as an opinion – preferably a *low* opinion – about yourself and your virtues? This is the very tactic Screwtape urges on Wormwood.

Draw his attention to himself … get him, if he is intelligent trying to think he's not; or she, if she's pretty, trying to convince herself she's plain. You see, they know this isn't entirely true and that gets them more confused and more pre-occupied with themselves.

Once our thinking starts revolving around the questions of whether I'm the most charming, intelligent, prettiest or wittiest person in the room then I'm certainly not the most humble. Echoes of 'Mirror, Mirror on the wall who is the humblest – no *prettiest* of them all?' The humble man keeps off the subject of his own value altogether.

Cardinal Newman once defined a gentleman as 'one who thinks of all the company'. This is exactly the same with the humble man: someone who thinks of all the company and not of himself. The vain and conceited man, by contrast, wants all the company to notice and think of him. He wants praise and attention and is forever angling for it in a thousand little ways. We see these little 'attention devices' most noticeably in children.

Now, I feel sure there is a trap here somewhere. Are we to assume from this every effort to please others must be branded as pride on our part? Odd as it must sound, after what I've just said, the desire for and pleasure in being praised is not automatically pride. The child who is patted on the shoulder for doing his homework well or helping Mummy, the woman whose beauty is praised by her husband or fiancé, the saved soul to whom Christ says 'well done, good and faithful servant', are pleased and ought to be. Yes. For the pleasure here lies not in how good you are but in the fact that you have pleased someone you rightly wanted to please. The trouble begins when you pass from thinking 'I have pleased him; all is well', to thinking, like Little Jack Horner, 'What a fine person I must be to have done it.' This brings us back to the high or low opinion you have of yourself; and with it pre-occupation with self and with praise and attention from others.

All this spells out a very simple principle: The Principle of Indirection. It means there are many virtues, many good things in life that cannot be obtained by striving for them directly; for, directly you do so they elude you. Humility is one of them; praise is another. Directly you try to be humble by putting it on, by proclaiming to everyone you are nobody, it becomes 'put-on' and that, as we know, is the putting-off type of humility we call humbug. The humble man is not thinking about his humility. He is not thinking about himself at all – or as little as possible.

It is the same with praise. Once you start seeking praise directly, all you'll get from others is flattery. It is the unsolicited, the indirect remarks that are true praise and the true reward of any virtue or merit we may have. Something of the paradox comes out in those words of our Lord: 'He who finds his life shall lose it, and he who loses his life shall find it.'

C. S. Lewis, who is a great exponent of this principle, makes a good deal of it in his autobiography, *Surprised by Joy*. The theme of his life story is that, without seeking joy directly, he found himself constantly being surprised by it. You can't *put-on* joy; you might pretend to be joyful but it's not the same. You can't go down the town and purchase joy. It has to come indirectly, by surprise. The virtue of joy, for after all it is a virtue, a gift of the Holy Spirit, comes in being able to find joy in the simple and humble things of life.

Love is another virtue of this principle of indirection. Love is at its best where it means absorption in the other and obliviousness of oneself. That is why being in love does something for you. It takes you out of yourself. Phew! What a joy that is. The very word 'ecstatic' which I used to describe both the bliss of lovers and the trance of the mystic comes from the latin word *ecstasis* which means 'standing outside' yourself. The more you can maintain this outward looking stance the better it is and the happier you will be. And we're back again with self-forgetfulness. Once our gaze turns inwards and you become introverted and preoccupied with self (to the exclusion of others) you cheat yourself of the very things you seek.

That is why Screwtape urges Wormwood to get the patient thinking and worrying about himself – virtues or vices, doesn't matter, feelings, states of mind. Christ wants to get our minds off such questions; even our sins, once repented, must be forgotten. Seek first the kingdom of God and all these other things will be yours without the asking – directly.

Summerland (indirection)

33rd Sunday, Ordinary Time (1975)

L ast week, I was speaking about the Principle of Indirection. Now a parable is an interesting application of this principle. A parable is a story about something which is not itself the point. The point, purpose, moral of the story is to draw your attention to something in your own life. The classic use of this kind of story is the parable used by Nathan in the Old Testament (2 Sam 11). Briefly, what happened was this. King David fell in love with Uriah the Hittite's wife Bathsheba. And so as to have her as his own wife, he arranged for Uriah, a soldier, to be put where the battle was fiercest. And he was killed and David took Bathsheba for his wife. Nathan the prophet then comes along and tells David a story – a parable in fact. There was a rich man who had hundreds of sheep and a poor man who had one lambkin that was as dear to him as an only child. One day a visitor called in to see the rich man. The rich man instead of killing one of his own sheep to feast the friend had the poor man's sheep taken from him and killed. 'What do you think of that?' asked Nathan. David was livid. 'The man who did this deserves to die', he exclaimed. Nathan replied, 'That man is you!' Had Nathan made a direct charge against David, he would not have acknowledged it. But seeing it in the other context he realised what he had done and repented.

Anyone familiar with the Gospels will know how frequently Our Lord had recourse to parables to get his message across. Consequently, by way of commenting on today's parable about the talents, I'm going to tell you a modern parable.

Not many years ago, on an island not very far away which depended very heavily for its livelihood on holidaymakers, a brilliant and ambitious scheme was thought up that would solve, once and for all, the miseries of bad weather on holiday. In this one, fantastic building was contained all that a holidaymaker could possibly desire in the way of entertainment for himself and his family. On its brightly-coloured floors there was room for 5,000 people. It was fairyland in real life. It offered talent contests, pop music, community singing, bingo, pin tables, deck games, bars and restaurants. It had a sundome and saunas. The children had their own theatre, fun fair and discotheque, as well as the traditional Punch and Judy show. Just close your eyes and imagine it all on a rainy day. Heaven on earth? The building was finished in 1971 and for two years it was a roaring success. It more than justified the hopes and expectations of the planners. Then one day in August, when everyone was saying, 'How quiet and peaceful it all is', the day of reckoning came. 3,000 people were happily occupying themselves within its walls when a fire broke out and with terrifying rapidity swept through the building. Fifty people died in the stampede that followed and over a hundred were injured.

No doubt, you will have recognised the story as the story about the fire at Summerland on the Isle of Man. In that sense it doesn't tell you anything you don't already know. And, if you think about it, none of Our Lord's parables say anything his listeners didn't already know. However, by telling you this story in a definite context – the context of what I've been saying about the principle of indirection, and the context of the readings we've just heard – you know that there is a lesson to this story of Summerland. Therefore, let me explain the parable to you as I see it.

The disaster was the outcome of an accumulation of human errors, negligences and above all of what people failed to do. There was no single arch-villain of the piece in the same way as Hitler could be reckoned the arch-villain of World War II.

But everyone connected with it, in their eagerness to achieve heaven on earth, slipped up (or down) in one way or another. The architects failed to vet important decisions of their assistants. The Douglas corporation was prevailed upon to waive significant by-laws because the building couldn't be strictly classified as coming under 'theatre regulations'. As a result common sense standards were applied. The material for the roof was only thought to be non-combustible. In fact, it was so combustible that workers took offcuts home to light fires with. Basically, however, the overall fire precautions were adequate. The fire chief said after the fire that there had been enough time to evacuate the building three times over. *But*:

In addition to the negligences of the builders there were those of the staff. No proper fire drill had been worked out. From the first to the last no Fire Alarm was sounded. Only when the fire was out of control did someone phone the fire brigade. The attendants were reluctant to take seriously the alarm raised by the first people to notice it. To reassure those of his audience who had seen the smoke the compère quipped about a 'fire in a chip pan' and the organist said 'I'll play the Blue Danube and put it out.' People making for the exits returned to their seats.

It all sounds so like the Lord's parables on the last things. Plenty of warning but no heed taken of them. Moreover, in this short but tragic chapter of human endeavour is revealed the unenviable predicament of our lot. It's more than a dilemma between complacency, excessive caution and excessive risk. With complacency there is the risk of saying what does it matter, we've got to be sensible. Alternatively, one can be too cautious and for fear of every imaginable consequence stick rigidly to the letter of the law. Finally, there is the need to take sensible risks in order to meet the challenges of life. I came across a book recently called *Courage to fail*. It was about people suffering from defective adrenal glands. It's a relatively new field of medicine and so much of the treatment is still at an experimental stage. Risks have to be taken with as much caution as possible but they still have to be taken if progress is to be made.

The Summerland parable brings the parable of the talents up to date. Putting your five talents to good use *alone* is not sufficient. It doesn't matter who you are or what you are doing: whether you are an architect, a civil servant, a fire inspector or an attendant, every little negligence or failure to act responsibly, whether we like it or not, is contributing by accumulation of such mistakes to a day of reckoning that is going to cost lives and even, souls. That soul may be yours!

Bonfire

Feast of All Saints (1981)

It is almost certainly true to say that more people in Britain are more likely to know the importance of the 5th November than the 1st. 'Please do remember the 5th of November', so the Guy Fawkes jingle goes. But how are we to remember that November 1st is All Saints – or, its older name, All Hallows, a word derived from 'hallow' to make holy. 'Hallowed be thy name.' One unfortunate kid thought it was 'Harold be thy name.'

One reason why I mentioned Guy Fawkes night is because the bonfire that it is traditional to have is an excellent symbol of the Church and the holiness of its members. A symbol is not telling you something you don't know or don't do already. What it's doing is helping you to appreciate the knowledge you already have. It is the same if you have a close brush with death in a car accident. We all know we are mortal – in theory – but it needs just such a narrow miss to bring home that fact in a rather uncomfortable way.

What is the first thing that comes to mind when you say 'bonfire'? The bonfire needs lots of wood and rubbish before you can have one. That's the human race: a pile of dead faggots rotting on the ground.

The next thing you need to have for a bonfire is a light. No light, no fire. All the gold in China won't light it but one match will. Christ is the light who starts the fire. He gathered his disciples and apostles together and set light to them. He said, 'I have come to cast fire on the earth.'

There is one thing quite certain about a bonfire, you can't have it indoors. It has to be outside. This is so true of the church. Many people like to think that their religion is a private affair between themselves and God. They box it in and try to live in the box. That's not what the church is.

We can get a better idea of the church from the effects of a bonfire on those around. It is a source of light and warmth. On a dark November night no one could see who was there or what they were doing. This is what the church does, it helps people to see each other in a new way and love them in a new way. It also guides them. 'The church is the light of the world.' A young lad was once asked what a deacon was. He answered, 'You put him on a high hill and when the enemy comes you light him.' The bonfire also spreads its warmth. A bonfire is alive and burning. Even the damp and wet wood catches alight once the centre is hot enough.

It reminds me of the two disciples who met up with the Risen Jesus on the way to Emmaus. Their comment after he had vanished was 'Were not our hearts burning within us as he spoke?' A good bonfire is contagious.

To get a really good blaze going you must have plenty of wind. The more the wind the better the blaze. The wind in the church is the Holy Spirit. If you remember at the first Pentecost there was the sound of a mighty wind blowing through the house and tongues of fire appeared on the heads of the apostles. And when they went out the effect on the bystanders was incredible – three thousand asked to be baptised.

A bonfire is noisy and crackles and even roars. Somehow, a bonfire is fun; it is alive and has to be kept alive. You can't sit around eating roasted chestnuts for long. Everyone is needed to bring more fuel to feed the flames. The church is not going to be what Christ wanted it to be if everyone sits at home eating his chestnuts. We must be giving of ourselves, our time, our gifts, our all. I say 'it's fun', but I don't mean you can play with fire: you can get burned. Religion is not kids' stuff. I know it can generate more heat than light sometimes. Sparks fly too! But just because fire burns we don't refuse to have anything to do with it. We treat it with the respect it deserves.

The final point to notice about a bonfire is what happens to the wood. When the wood burns it produces flames and these flames go leaping and dancing up to heaven. If the wood is not burnt it rots and sinks into the ground. Isn't that like our life in the church? In the church, in the bonfire, the dead wood of our lives, the rubbish, is transformed through Jesus' action in the sacraments into a burning flame that enables us to fly heavenwards when we finally die.

You, then, are the bonfire – or the wood that makes up the bonfire, the church. *Really* belong to that fire so that others may come, through you, to experience the love and the warmth, the hope and reassurance, the message of life that Christ came to bring.

We need saints and heroes

Feast of All Saints (1999)

In early life, we decided what we wanted to be by observing people and careers we admired. As we grow older, we need good examples to spur us on. Everyone knows how hard it is to keep up any sort of standard in life. We all suffer from the 'slipping socks syndrome'. There is no shortage of texts urging us to pull up our socks. Scripture is full of them. Words from Revelation come to mind:

> I know what you have done; I know that you are neither hot nor cold. How I wish you were one or the other! But because you are lukewarm, neither hot nor cold, I am going to spit you out of my mouth (Rev 3:15–16).

Words alone, however, invaluable though they are, are not enough: we need examples, models, and real live people to fire our imaginations.

Yet, there is a fine balance between being encouraged by them to try harder, and being discouraged by their very perfection, from trying at all. We need their perfection, but we need their human frailty too. I recall a story about Yehudi Menuhin; a brilliant musician if ever there was one. He used to go and play in the orchestra at the school for musicians he founded. One time he was playing a concerto with the pupils and somehow he got out of time. When they stopped, he turned to Jasmine and asked, 'Was I out of time, Jasmine?' 'You were a bar ahead of us, sir,' she replied. He took it extremely well.

Human wisdom and conceit always imagine that the holiness we aspire to means fame in the worldly sense. Padre Pio is very well known, but he was a very exceptional man. 'To whom more is given, more is expected.' St Paul frequently comes back to the fact that if we boast we must boast in the Lord and not in our own achievements. 'What have you that you have not received?' In Paul's way of thinking, nothing is excluded from God's purpose. His 'will is our sanctification' and God is able to draw good from everything that happens in our lives, even our sins and failures. Such is the competitive world we live in, we can't help thinking sanctity lies in great deeds, impressive miracles, long hours in prayer and mammoth fasts. Sanctity, as Thérèse observed, is more of a disposition of heart towards God and others: a disposition that can be demonstrated as easily by small actions, faithfully done, week in week out, as by some great deed done once.

However, we still need saints and heroes to goad us into action, to shake us out of our lethargy, to remind us that holiness is a reality, and above all, sin is also a reality. We mustn't shrug our shoulders over our sins, saying, 'What's the use of trying? It's my nature. I'm born that way.' That is precisely why we need people like Nelson Mandela and Mother Teresa. They make us sit up and try a bit harder. Success may (or may not) impress. Goodness, on the other hand, never fails to move us. Nelson Mandela is one of the most widely admired of all contemporary heroes. His struggles against apartheid and his years in prison, bring home the man's heroism. Greatness doesn't happen in a day. It demands tremendous fidelity to the small details of life. Mother Teresa was another amazing person. You can see from the number of sisters in her organisation how powerfully she drew people to her cause – even great people. Her words to Princess Diana sum up her wisdom: 'You know you couldn't do my work and I couldn't do yours. We are both working for God. Let us do something beautiful for God.'

Just what St Paul says:

> My brothers and sisters, fill your minds with those things that are good and that deserve praise: things that are true, noble, right, pure, lovely and honourable. Put into practice what you learnt and received from me, both from my words and from my actions. And the God of peace be with you (Phil 4:8–9).

The church has continued down the ages to define and remind us of sanctity wherever it appears. It is not something new. Consider the shrines and relics of the martyrs and saints. They have been around for nearly two thousand years. We need heroes. We need saints. I urge you to devote some time today recalling stories and people who have inspired you and helped you along the road, helped you to bear some trial, fight some weakness, strive after higher things. We need *heroes*. The Reader's Digest always manages to find stories of heroic achievements and feats of endurance. They are invariably stimulating. Yet we need *saints* even more. They help connect what happens in our lives with God and his holy will. We need places of pilgrimage where saints have lived, we need their writings and their prayers to guide and lift us up above the ordinary. We need their feasts to brighten our daily journey and to remind us of their teaching and example. We need their intercession to procure some of the many graces we call out for. I don't think a day has passed when there has been no votive candle burning at the shrine of Blessed Cyprian. So many are the urgent needs in so many people's lives. Above all, we need this feast of All Saints: the feast of those men and women we have known and whose lives and wisdom have remained and will remain with us all our days.

Sermon for St Benedict

Feast of Saint Benedict (1969)

Love drives out fear.

St Benedict assures us that if we persevere in the degrees of humility 'we will presently arrive at that love of God which casts fear out'. He is basing himself on St John's first epistle, where we read:

> Love has no room for fear, and, indeed, love drives out fear when it is perfect love, since fear involves the prospect of punishment. The man who is still afraid has not yet reached the full measure of love (1 Jn 4:18).

The fear both St John and St Benedict have in mind is the fear of hell and the last judgement. Both show that if we love and trust our Saviour enough we need have no fears.

St Benedict's line of thought is not too easy to follow. Fear has been given an important part in his degrees of humility, so why should he close the chapter by saying love casts it out? In the first degree 'a monk always keeps the *fear* of God before his eyes … remembering that life everlasting is prepared for those who *fear* God'. And in the 12th degree 'a monk must ever think of the guilt of his sins and imagine himself already present before the terrible judgement seat of God'. Presumably he does not intend these degrees to be regarded as so many booster rockets which are jettisoned as we go on up. I think he means what Dr Martin Luther King once said: 'Normal fear protects and motivates; abnormal fear paralyses and poisons our life. Our problem (he said) is not to rid ourselves of fear but to harness it and master it.' And the best way to do that, St Benedict would add, is by love. Consequently there will always be fears in our life, but as we grow in love we will become less afraid of them. Or, to put it in St John's words, 'The man who is still afraid has not yet reached the full measure of love.'

There are many things we fear in life. What Jeffery Emerson said is all too true: 'He has not learned the lesson of life who does not everyday surmount a fear.' Fear, as we all know, is the avoidance of an unwanted evil. One has only to think of a few of the things we avoid to see how fear enters our life. We avoid people, duties and jobs. We also try to avoid germs, although not always successfully. We avoid speaking in public because it is an ordeal that makes us nervous. And unless we can force ourselves to see and love the good in it, both for ourselves and for others, wild horses won't get us near the rostrum. This particular example is not directed at anyone in particular – implying that they are funking it. It cuts both ways. If all were obliged to read or sing, the danger would be for the listeners, and the ordeal (to be avoided at all costs) of listening to so-and-so read or preach.

Avoidance, then, is one of the disguises fear dresses up in. Another, equally regular visitor, is 'loss of nerve'. Gilbert Murray started off this now well-known dictum. He explained how the Greeks were extremely confident in man's ability to create a completely intelligible world. This classic faith was shaken, and men turned to God to do what they no longer felt confident to do. It was, in a sense, a 'failure of nerve'. Today, the *world* has recovered its nerve and is boldly going ahead. This has had the reverse effect, if not on the Church, at least on her members. When you come to think of it, failure, or loss of nerve, is one of the most prevalent and disturbing features of our present day church. Pope John XXIII is one of the notable exceptions; he did much to restore the church's confidence in herself. Popes and Councils, however, can help but they cannot do it for the individual Christian. Fewer vocations, more departures, uneasy conservatives, and discontented progressives, all indicate the presence of nerve failure to some extent. Either things aren't going fast enough, or every change is another step in the wrong direction.

We meet this, here, in our own monastery. People do not leave because they are happy and contented with the life, but rather because they have lost their nerve for it. This unsettles others, because it casts suspicion and doubt on the value of such a life. Nor is it easy for young people to hold on to their nerve. Today, when a career and status in a successful and prosperous world are so attractive – or so the adverts would have us believe – a monastery can offer a man nothing that can be favourably compared. What is more, the nature of obedience means that a man's future is not finally decided by himself. He has to face the 'father complex', as it has been called, that is, the prospect of remaining a child under another man all one's life. It's not always the case. One man, here, who admittedly left eventually, was asked whether he liked his job: 'I wouldn't be doing it if I didn't,' he replied.

Young or old, it requires tremendous nerve to go on at times and not to yield or be perturbed by the thousand and one niggardly fears that assail us each day. Apart from the more serious fears about personal fulfilment and character development in a closed society, the worries of the daily routine are quite enough to unnerve the best of us. To be able to go on doing the same old things year after year requires a nerve. And one has to have just as much nerve to change all these old ways of doing things.

The picture is a depressing one, and yet it is the true picture if we once allow our fears to get the better of us. If fear dominates our actions then avoidance will be in high relief, because fear is negative. People we don't like, we avoid. It's quite simple: either ignore them or be stern, irritable and unsympathetic and you can be sure people will keep away. Jobs or changes we don't like, we avoid. To avoid changes ... need I say more? We are so wise at the gentle art of self-defence.

If, on the other hand, love drives away our fears, or at least enables us to bear with them, then we shall never lose our zest for life and all that it entails. Love is particularly important when it demands sacrifice. Fear never moved anyone, except to run away. Our Lord was afraid of his Passion, but his *love* of us kept him to his purpose. It was not just the suffering he feared, but the triumph of his enemies, the failure of his cause and his ambitions, the desertion by his friends, and the rejection of his Father by the Jews. We may have as many similar fears. And to adhere to God's will in the face of them will demand more and more love. Only love can build dykes strong enough to hold back the floods of fears that menace us. And it is interesting how this theme runs through the Bible, the psalms especially. In spite of all the forebodings of trouble predicted by the prophets, love and confidence in Yahweh remain on top. Although all my cherished hopes were to come to nothing, Habakkuk says, 'yet I will rejoice in Yahweh. I will exult in God my Saviour. Yahweh my Lord is my strength'. An old adage will provide a fitting conclusion: 'Fear knocked at the door; love answered; there was no one there.'

Sermon for St Bernard

Feast of St Bernard (1975)

You have come hither as I suppose, to hear the word of God. At least I cannot conceive any other motive that would account for the presence of this eager multitude. I approve your desire of edification and congratulate you on your good disposition. 'Blessed are they who hear the word of God', says our Saviour, but he adds:- (mark it well) 'and keep it'.

de Conversione

The year was 1140 and Bernard, ten years older than his century, was passing through Paris. Bishop Stephen asked him to address the students of the city in the hope that he might bring about some improvement in their manner of living. Our Father was reluctant. It was not his custom to speak in public unless some grave necessity required it. However, it seems he had some vision or inspiration during the night which changed his mind. He had no difficulty in holding the attention of his audience. Reading the sermon, one is surprised to find him being sarcastic in places:

Slave of ambition, have you succeeded at last in obtaining the dignity so long coveted? Take care lest you lose it again. Slave of avarice, have you filled up your coffers? Guard them well or they may be stolen. Thrifty husbandman, have your fields produced an abundant harvest? Pull down your barns and build greater ones; change them from square to round and say to your soul, Thou has many things laid up for years. But the time will come when you shall hear the dreaded judgement: Thou fool, this day they have required thy soul of thee.

The sermon was much admired and applauded and they all wanted him to speak again. But our Father regarded it as a failure because no one was converted. He was so upset by this apparent failure that when he reached his room in the house where he was lodging, he burst into sobs and groans audible enough to be heard outside. The Archdeacon whose house it was asked Rainald what was the matter? Rainald explained that Bernard was so intent on bringing sinners back to God that when there were no fruits of conversion, he thinks he has lost God's favour. God seems to have reassured Bernard at prayer for he preached again the following day. This time his words went home and even during the sermon three young men came forward. At the conclusion twenty followed him back to Clairvaux.

These two sermons are known to us as the Treatise on Conversion. What is so interesting about it is that it provides us with some idea of how St Bernard preached and managed to persuade people to leave all and enter Clairvaux. It is the same when reading the Acts of the Apostles: the sermons reported there are those which moved thousands to embrace the Christian way of life. Bernard's technique is direct to the point:

> It is indeed hard to be virtuous situated as you are here. For chastity is not safe in the midst of delights, nor is humility in the midst of wealth nor devotion in the midst of distractions, nor truth in the midst of idle gossip nor charity in the midst of this wicked world. Flee, therefore, out of Babylon, flee and let everyone save his own soul; flee, I say, to the cities of refuge where you may do penance for the past, obtain grace in the present, and look with confidence to receive the crown of glory in the future ... Be not discouraged by the austerity of a penitential life. The sufferings of this time are not worthy to be compared with either the sins of the past which shall be forgiven you, or with the grace of consolation which shall be infused into your souls, or with the glory that is to come.

The extraordinary part about it all was that the life he was inviting them to embrace was nothing if not hard and spartan. Nor did he ever mitigate its austerities to make it more attractive. At the same time, he could write to the anxious parents of a young monk:

> Do not be worried about the frail health of your son. I will be to him like a father and a mother, both a brother and a sister, and I will so temper and arrange all things for him that his soul may profit without his body suffering.

The humanity and realism of our Father can be seen not only in touching incidents like this, but also from the occasional asides in his sermons:

> I wish some of you sitting there would think of the respect you owe to your superiors and bear in mind that by needlessly bothering them you make yourselves tiresome even to the citizens of heaven. You know how seldom I have an hour free from visitors or someone wanting to see me. Yet I mention this with diffidence lest some brethren might hide their trouble beyond their capacity to endure it for fear of disturbing me. (In Cant. 52, 7.)

Another aside reveals more the sort of grumbles that Bernard did not want to be troubled with – he is commenting on the text:

> I treasured wisdom more than health and beauty: 'if more than health and beauty, how much more than pleasures and shamefulness? What does it profit a monk to restrain himself from pleasures if he is always bothering about the appearances of his food and how it is served? He says: 'Vegetables give me wind, cheese weighs down my stomach, milk is bad for my head, my chest suffers if I drink water, beans make me melancholy, leeks heat my blood, fish from ponds and muddy water spoil my complexion.' Oh, I beg you, have pity on your peace of mind and consider just a little the good of your soul.'

Occasionally, our Father's temper got the better of him, which is hardly surprising in view of his constant fatigue and bad health. In a letter he admits: 'The other day, I got really furious with one of the brothers and angrily told him to get out of the monastery. He left for one of the granges' (Letter 73). Our Father regretted this action and goes on to tell how he invited the brother back after his council had advised him to do so. He had put the matter to them because 'I could not trust my own judgement in the affair owing to my natural feelings about it.' Bernard was well aware of the strength of his own impulses and generally tried to act in consultation with others. Although he was frequently absent from the monastery it was always at the command of a higher superior. It would be a rewarding study to find out exactly how much our Father did on his own initiative and how much in response to advice or appeal. We know that his mandate to preach the Crusade only extended to France. Had he limited it to that and not gone on to Germany the results might well have been less disastrous.

St Bernard often emphasised the need to be a fool for Christ's sake. Well, he was fooled well and truly himself once. Nicolas of Montieramey was Bernard's secretary. He also seems to have done a shuttle service and acted as secretary for Peter the Venerable of Cluny. Our Father refers in a letter to 'my Nicolas who is also yours, sends his love'. Occasionally Nicolas took it upon himself to add his own affectionate greetings as a postscript. Peter in a letter asks for the loan of Nicolas to cheer him up. Then, a sinister note appears in Bernard's letters: 'I am in danger from false brethren. Many forged letters have gone out under my seal' (Ep 354). And when he finds out who the culprit is his indignation knows no bounds: 'A serpent has deceived me! A doubled-faced, cunning wretch, completely devoid of any righteousness, an enemy to his own soul …' (Ep 339). After the storm had subsided, he ruefully recounts:

> Nicolas has left us, leaving a trail of slime. He was not one of us. I knew for some time what sort of man he was, but I was waiting either for God to convert him, or for him to betray himself like Judas: and this is what happened.

Our Father felt very sore about it. One can only wonder in retrospect whether Bernard and Peter didn't bring it upon themselves by spoiling him with their attentions and letting him take liberties with their seals? On the other hand it reveals the complete trust and real friendship that existed between our Father and his monks.

These few words are hardly what you could call a sermon. They are rather like passing round a few snapshots from the family album, some random pictures of our Father, St Bernard.

Sermon for Sts Peter and Paul

Feast of Sts Peter and Paul (1996)

Some children were asked to write down: 'Things I would like to do when I grow up.' Most copybooks next day listed things like: 'help the poor' or 'have a family' or 'be rich'. One nine-year-old had the following list: 'Have a job. Drink a pint. Have a car. See the world. Have my own money. Wear the clothes I like.' If that doesn't speak volumes for what a child is learning from the media nothing does. That's where the *real* education is being done. The irony of it is: how many nineteen-year-olds are no wiser than they were at nine!

One thing is certain: our culture encourages us to be self-sufficient. We have a deep desire to be independent, strong and free. Some other children were asked, next time they came into school, to bring something which symbolised a hymn they liked. One child came in carrying a torch. Another brought a cob. Yet another clutched an ice cream. The first said the torch was a symbol of 'Lead kindly light'. The next said the cob was a symbol of 'In bread we bring you, Lord'. The other had them guessing until he explained the ice cream was something he was 'keeping tight hold of'. Modern young people may well want to keep tight hold of their independence and self-sufficiency; eventually, however, they will discover how illusive these are. For a whole variety of reasons we find ourselves saying, even if not in so many words: 'I cannot manage, I need help, I need light (the kindly light) of Jesus.' In a word, I need to know that I am not and cannot be my own saviour.

Both Sts Peter and Paul discovered this in their different ways. The experience of their weakness not the knowledge of their strength was what led them to a deeper understanding of Jesus. 'I know him whom I have believed', 'I am the least of all', 'When I am weak then I am strong.' How often St Paul goes out of his way to express his appreciation for all those who helped him, for those who gave money, for those who ran errands for him and helped him in prison. But Paul was as independent as anyone could be. He would weave tents all night rather than be beholden to anyone for his livelihood. He was an extraordinary man. He was a great fundraiser, he was a captivating preacher and teacher, an untiring missionary. His grasp of the mysteries of the faith is astounding, not to mention his mystical experiences in the seventh heaven. Against this apparent success story is the story of his sufferings, of the opposition he met with, of his imprisonments, his shipwrecks. All things he writes off as 'mere nothings compared to the glory that is to come', 'slight momentary afflictions'. We have to have only some minor hardship, one dull day and we are for giving up.

Such is the power and dynamism of St Paul that one almost finds it hard to match anything similar in St Peter's life. Comparisons are odious. Peter's life and example are probably more what we need than the charismatic life of St Paul.

It seems to me that we are always at a disadvantage when we reflect on the lives of great men and women. Hindsight in the study of peoples' lives has one great drawback: it implies that they had all their greatness and ability at the start, that they knew exactly what was going to happen, and that they knew the way to go. But it never was and never is like that. When Peter met Jesus by the lake of Tiberias, he gave his 'Yes' in answer to Jesus' call to follow him, but he had no idea of the consequences. What ideas he had were most likely mistaken, especially if he thought Jesus was to be the liberator of Israel. Even on the shores of the same lake, after the Resurrection, Peter was only told his future in veiled terms:

> Truly I say to you, when you were young, you girded yourself and walked where you would; but when you are old, you will stretch out your hands, and another will gird you and carry you where you would not go (Jn 21:18).

How true for many an old person as they are forced to leave their homes and go into some form of care. We all want to remain independent. We all want to know what lies ahead. We all want to be masters of our own destiny but at the end of the day another will gird us and take us where we would not go.

Not only did Peter have to live with uncertainty. His whole life seems to take a course between triumphs and trials, success and failures. Fidelity never came by a simple succession of achievements.

No sooner had the miracle of Cana taken place, 'when Jesus manifested his glory, and his disciples believed in him' than a few days later Jesus was driving out the buyers and sellers and talking about 'destroying this temple and in three days rebuilding it' (Jn 2:19). The apostles must have thought that this was a strange way of inaugurating his mission. Time passed and things seem to be going their way until the miracle of the feeding the 5,000. This was it. A man who could do that sort of thing was the man to be following. This was the kind of manifestation of power that was called for. Then comes the sting, the test. This time it was the teaching on the bread of life: 'He who eats my flesh and drinks my blood' (Jn 6:22–70). That really shook his followers. How could this Jesus, the son of Joseph, whose father and mother we know, talk like this? And they all began to desert him. The fidelity of the disciples was shaken much more deeply this time. It was a trial, a test that produced Peter's 'Lord, to whom else shall we go? You have the words of eternal life' (Jn 6:68). Throughout his life and ours too, the human ideas we have of Jesus and his mission have to go. I know from my own experience, how down the years, those simple words of Peter have been a sort of *quo vadis?* (Where are you going, Lord?). They turned me round and faced me back to Jesus. Of all the other possibilities I could think of, all the other roads I was tempted to turn down, none had the security or sureness of the way Jesus was leading.

Were there time, one could follow up the pattern in Peter's life of little successes, followed by upsets and trials that drew from him ever deeper love and faith and taught him the true meaning of following Jesus. Even his denial of Jesus you could say was the hardest lesson he had to learn.

Here then is a message to learn from the lives of Peter and Paul. We all want to be strong and free. Like the nine-year-old who wanted to do his own thing. Yet, eventually we discover that self-sufficiency is not the object of our search. For a whole variety of reasons we find ourselves saying, even if not in so many words: 'I cannot manage on my own.' 'Lord, to whom else shall we turn? You have the message of eternal life.'

Sermon for Sts Peter and Paul

Feast of Sts Peter and Paul (2002)

What marvels the Lord worked for us; indeed we were glad

If you ever mention some well-known person, be they famous people, or saints – take St Padre Pio or Sir Bob Geldof – you inevitably begin to ask yourself what great deeds must they have done to be awarded these distinctions? I always remember one old chap who regularly protested his innocence to me by saying, 'I ain't done nothing, Father.' I used to think to myself, 'I wish you had', but, obviously, what he was protesting was his innocence: he hadn't done anything wrong. I was wishing he had done some external deeds of good.

As our thoughts turn to Sts Peter and Paul today we begin to ponder on their great missionary deeds, their zeal in spreading the news of Jesus right across the Roman Empire, their heroic deaths and witness to their faith. In other words, all the kind of things by which we measure greatness in a person. In this frame of mind, we would have expected the readings to pick out a particular occasion in their lives when they did something great. Well, we were disappointed. The readings suggest another thought; they prompt us to look beyond what great deeds they did to what great deeds God did for them and through them.

The first reading describes Peter's remarkable liberation from prison. Herod, in beheading James, had found a vote-winner, and decided to do the same for Peter, whom he accordingly imprisoned with state-of-the-art security systems in place to ensure he didn't escape. Meanwhile, though, the Church was praying for him; and when that happens, you need to watch out – the unexpected happens. So unexpected was it, that Peter thought he was dreaming – and so did the maid who answered the door. It is only at the end that he comes to his senses, and is able to say, 'Now I know the truth that the Lord has sent his angel.'

This is the mood of the psalm. 'I shall bless the Lord at all times, his praise ever on my lips. Glorify the Lord with me ... This poor man called, the Lord heard him.' Psalm 33 is often used for a responsorial psalm, as it is so characteristic of life. We are celebrating what wonderful things the Lord does for us, rather than what we have done for him.

The second reading likewise displays immense confidence in God. Paul was ready for off. My mother used to say her bags were packed, meaning she was ready and waiting for her heavenly call to leave this world. St Paul mentions these very people (who long for the Lord's coming) when he said, 'the crown of righteousness reserved for me, which the Lord, the righteous judge, will give to me on that Day; and not only to me but to *all* those who have longed for his Appearing' (2 Tim 4:8).

But the key words follow: 'The Lord *stood by me* and *gave me power*, so that through me the whole message might be proclaimed; and so I was rescued from the lion's mouth' (2 Tim 4:17). Peter was rescued from prison; Paul was rescued from the lion's mouth and did valiant work spreading the gospel, because the 'Lord stood by him and gave him power.' Here indeed is the wisdom of the Church apparent to us. Instead of leaving church downcast by hearing about all the great things Peter and Paul did and worried by the little we seem to do, we are forcibly reminded of the great things the Lord *did* for and through them – and will do 'for all those who have longed for his Appearing'.

Finally, see what happens in the Gospel. Jesus sits his apostles down and tries to give them a theology class when what they were worried about was who was the greatest among them.

'Who am I?' He asks. Furtive glances among the apostles, what does he mean? [David Beckham? Bob Geldof? Lloyd Webber?] Then Peter throws caution to the wind, 'You're the Messiah, the Son of the Living God.' Well done, Peter! Knowing smiles all round. Of course, yes! Peter saved them from an embarrassing moment, that time. Then, just as Peter was beginning to congratulate himself for having passed his SATS (college admission exams), Jesus calmly went on: 'Flesh and blood did not reveal this to you, but my Father in heaven.' Then, and only then, did Jesus hand out the award: 'You are Peter, and upon this rock I will build my Church' (Mt 16:18).

Peter and Paul ain't done nothing, in a manner of speaking; it was the wonderful deeds the Lord did through them, and will continue to do through *all those who long for his Appearing*. To my mind, one of the most profound things St Thérèse ever said was when she was dying. She was feeling low, thinking about how little she had achieved or could achieve in such a short life. Then her spirits revived and she remarked:

> When I get to heaven, I wont dare turn and point to all the things I have done or not done, as if they were what made me worthy of a place in heaven, I will simply turn and point at Jesus and say: 'See what he has done for me.' And Our Lady said exactly the same: 'He that is mighty has done great things for me.'

That is what we are celebrating today on this feast of Sts Peter and Paul: 'the marvels God worked for them' and through them for us. 'Now, think what he has done for *you*' (Tobias).

'Come closer'

Feast of the Assumption (1993)

> *'I kept looking at her as hard as I could,' said St Bernadette,*
> *'and she kept looking steadily at me.'*

The thousands who had flocked to the grotto at Lourdes on that February morning in 1858 saw nothing, only Bernadette. Their eyes were fixed on the slip of a girl, but the look on her face assured them of an unseen presence.

Like we would have been, they were eager to know more. They asked her: 'Tell us, does the Lady look at anybody but yourself?' 'Oh, yes', replied Bernadette, 'she looks all round the crowd, and stops at some, as if they were old, familiar friends.'

Today we keep the Feast of Mary's Assumption. The Eastern Church calls it the Dormition – the sleeping of Our Lady. Because Mary was without sin, God freed her from the greatest consequence of sin – death – and assumed (took up) Mary's body and soul directly into heaven at the end of her life. Mary's assumption is a gift Jesus won for us all by his own death and resurrection, that is why the second reading speaks of the victory Christ won and how we shall all one day share in that victory. Mary's assumption is a tremendous source of hope to us all.

It is because of this hope which she gives us that we are always ready to learn more about her. Let us then ask Bernadette what else the Lady did? Her reply is very significant. She said:

1) The Lady looked at me;
2) She smiled at me;
3) She said, 'Come closer.'

Half our spirituality, half of our faith is simply a question of being aware, being more attentive. In the name of Mary, I invite you, on this Feast of the Assumption, to be more aware of your Mother's love, your

Mother Mary's loving and caring look. This is not something fanciful; this is a fact. It was Jesus' dying request: 'Mother, look! your son.' John stood there for us all. And from that moment on Our Lady has been looking, looking after her children. Looks say so much. Look with love. Look with pity. A reproachful look. When Peter had denied Jesus three times, Jesus only had to look at him for Peter to realise what he had done wrong.

St Bernadette then said, 'The Lady smiled at me.' We need our heavenly Mother's approval just as children do their earthly mother's. It's the mother's smile that reassures the child. It is extraordinary, isn't it, how one of the first things a baby learns to do is to smile; long before it can talk. And it learns it from seeing its parents smile. That our Lady smiled at Bernadette is very significant. Had it been a frown then we could have been worried. We know, however, that our Lady wasn't an indulgent mother whose children could do no wrong. On one occasion she failed to appear, and told Bernadette afterwards why. Because there had been some evil-minded people in the crowd.

Our Lady looked at her, smiled at her, and said: 'Come closer'. That means, come closer to her and to her Son; as the hymn puts it: 'that we may have a closer walk with Jesus'.

What is it that makes so many keep at a safe distance and not come closer? Why do they remain uncertain, hesitant, uncommitted and uninvolved? Mary is there, welcoming us, looking at us with her loving smile: what could be more inviting? I suppose it was the same on Calvary. The people watched from afar, at a safe distance, waiting to see what happened, which way things would go.

Yet, one of the most basic truths of the Bible is that God comes near to his people. As the psalmist says: 'He is close to the broken-hearted.' He came to live among us as a man. He could hardly have come closer than that. He comes close to us, why can't we come closer to him?

Today, then, whilst we are celebrating Mary's homecoming, her journey's end in the love of God, it is not with the despairing thought: 'It's alright for some'. Mary is not an infinite distance away, totally out of touch with all that is happening in this vale of tears. She is closer to us than ever, even as she is closer to Jesus than ever. She remains our Mother. She is still looking at us, smiling at us and urging us to come closer. And, we, in our turn, must 'keep our eyes', as St Paul says, 'fixed on things above where Christ is'. That is how we will come closer and become more faithful followers of her Son. 'Holy Mary, Mother of God, pray for us sinners, now, and at the hour of our death. Amen.'

Best man

Feast of St John the Baptist (1981)

The bride is only for the bridegroom; and yet the bridegroom's friend who stands there and listens is glad when he hears the bridegroom's voice. The same joy I feel and now is complete. He must grow greater, I must grow smaller (Jn 3:29–30).

It is part of the aim of the fourth gospel to ensure John the Baptist received his proper place as the forerunner of Jesus, but no higher place than that. One thing is certain and this passage shows it – the admirable humility of John the Baptist. To begin with his ministry drew men to himself; he was the leader who gathered around him a band of followers. Then Jesus comes on the scene and John leads them to follow him. But, for John's earliest disciples this wasn't easy. They felt a loyalty to John and even resented the latecomers flocking over to Jesus. It would have been natural for John to have felt injured and by-passed. We all know how a friend's sympathy can be the worst possible thing for us. It can make us feel sorry for ourselves and encourage us to think we hadn't been treated very fairly.

John told his disciples three things. He told them he had never expected anything else. 'I am not the one you imagine me to be: that one is coming after me and I am not fit to undo his sandal' (Acts 13:25). He was only the voice crying in the wilderness.

The second point John made clear was that although he must grow less and less, he didn't mean by that doing less and less, taking less and less part in activities out of injured pride. 'All right, if they don't want me they won't have me' and walking off in a huff. In monastic life it is very easy to pull out of things from injured pride but under a veneer of justified righteousness. This John did not do.

St Paul was faced with a similar problem with his Corinthians. He writes:

You see the jealousy that I feel for you is God's own jealousy: I arranged for you to marry Christ so that I may give you away as a chaste virgin to this one husband. But the serpent with his cunning, seduced Eve and I am afraid that in the same way, your ideas may get corrupted and turned away from simple devotion to Christ (2 Cor 11:2).

His irritation is with Appollos and those others that were misleading them. He then says 'I think I am not in the least inferior to these superlative apostles.' His point is, it is not the man who commends himself but the man whom the Lord commends who is accepted (2 Cor 10:18). And he wasn't drawing men to himself but to Christ.

Finally, John used the figure of the 'friend of the bridegroom' to describe himself and his position. This is akin to our 'boatman' but in Jewish thought it was much more important. The 'friend' acted as the liaison between the bride and the groom; he arranged the wedding; he took out the invitations; he presided at the wedding feast. He also had special duties in connection with the bridal chamber. In none of this did he begrudge the bridegroom the bride. He knew he only had to bring them together and when he had accomplished his purpose he could rejoice.

The bride is only for the bridegroom; and yet the bridegroom's friend (the best man) who stands there and listens is glad when he hears the voice of the bridegroom. The same joy I feel and now is complete. He must grow greater, I must grow smaller.

'No man greater ...'

Feast of St John the Baptist (1984)

In a dream I had, a farm machine had broken down and I took it to the local garage to be seen to. Looking at it the mechanic soon pronounced his verdict – for verdict it was, in a sense. 'It's been assembled wrong', he said. And I thought, 'how strange. The same thing had happened only a short while before'. How often a breakdown seems to be the result of faulty assembly: wrong wires connected, or things badly adjusted or out of line. I can't believe it's only in the farming community that such things occur.

And it doesn't need a dream to bring home to our attention the way people are always ready to speak about the mistakes or misfortunes of another. Wrong assembly is someone else's fault. With our silage safely stored away, it's hard not to gloat over neighbouring farmers who are still cutting theirs. Or when you see one of their machines broken down. It only makes one wonder what they are saying about us when they see similar mishaps dogging our steps.

And yet, although this tendency to find fault seems to be a recognisable pattern of daily life, we still remain able to rise above such things and rejoice in the triumph of good.

This is a particularly Christian approach, for many of our feasts are celebrating the wonderful things God has done for us. One of the unique aspects of John the Baptist is that we not only celebrate the day of his martyrdom and heavenly birthday, we also celebrate his earthly birthday. Apart from Jesus and his Mother, no other person enjoys this distinction.

Whilst most men have the feeling of having been assembled wrong – 'Oh see in guilt I was born, a sinner was I conceived' (Ps 51) – with John the Baptist it was otherwise. The Divine Mechanic made doubly sure the herald of his Son was right from the start. 'The Lord called me before I was born, from my mother's womb he pronounced my name' (Isa 49:1). The responsorial psalm draws on Ps 138: 'For it was you who created my being, knit me together from my mother's womb.'

Don't get me wrong! I'm not saying there were only three people ever assembled right, and all the rest of us wrong. It wasn't the Divine Mechanic's fault that the Fall occurred and original sin took place. Pope Paul VI in his 'Credo of the People of God', says original sin which we inherit is not an actual sin which we ourselves commit.

> It is human nature, so fallen, so stripped of the grace that clothed it, injured in its own natural powers and subjected to the dominion of death, that it is transmitted to all men, and it is in this sense that every man is born in sin.

Into this broken down state of deformed humanity John the Baptist is born. This little child is to be a prophet of God, the Most High. He is to go ahead of the Lord to prepare his ways before him. He comes to point the way to the Divine Mechanic who is to reassemble us once more in the image and likeness of God. 'Behold, the Lamb of God who takes away the sin of the world.' That was the message. Today, we pause and think of the messenger and thank God for him.

The endurance of Blessed Cyprian

Blessed Cyprian Pilgrimage (2005)

I was wondering which characteristic of Blessed Cyprian I could single out for your attention this year. I remember Dom Ambrose spoke of his humility a few years ago and that was certainly one of Blessed Cyprian's outstanding virtues. There's another virtue that he had to a high degree and that was his endurance. To start with, his very name, Tansi, means just that. The full name is much longer and what it means is 'continue and go on bearing all the difficulties with patience and resignation to Divine Providence'. Everyone has a lot to bear or put up with in his/her lifetime. Tansi simply means: 'Be Patient, be resigned to God!'

Blessed Cyprian was the fourth and last son of the family and he was called Iwegbune – or Iwene for short. Iwene, or Egbunen in Aguleri dialect means, 'May I not be done to death by human malice, anger, or hatred; may man's fury not destroy me.' The name was based on a bitter experience Cyprian's father had had when he was unjustly imprisoned. He didn't want his son to give up easily but to be strong and endure. And Michael Iwene grew up to be a man of great courage and endurance.

Endurance is a quality that all the other virtues require because it's the quality which enables someone to hold on in there, to stick at it when the going gets tough. Endurance is what enables you to press on in spite of the weather, weaknesses of mind and body. It makes you put up with the 'downs' in life, put up and not give up with being human, limited and imperfect.

Endurance played a great part in the sufferings of Our Lord. It was also one of Blessed Cyprian's most notable strengths. A very early example of this endurance of his occurred as a teenager at the village school in 1914. John Mokwe, a fellow schoolboy, recounts how the master Mr Oraekie told Iwene to go and fetch water from the Ernie stream some distance away from the village. It was already getting dark

179

that evening and access to the stream was through a narrow, rugged, rocky pass. Iwene went off straight away; somehow he found his way to the stream and brought the water back. Iwene was full of courage. The same John Mokwe reckons that Iwene not only endured the rigid training but it actually formed his character for later and harder endurance tests.

In 1924 Michael Tansi was transferred to Aguleri to be headmaster of St Joseph's Primary School. He could easily have felt dispensed from the menial tasks of the school: but not Blessed Cyprian! He took part in all the domestic chores. He still did his cooking, laundry and the mission grounds. But never did he let this interfere with his daily visits to the Blessed Sacrament. Michael Idigo tells us this story:

> On one occasion I went to spend my holidays with him at Onitsha. The two of us shared between us the domestic duties. So while I pounded the boiled yam, he was busy making the sauce. When the meal was ready, I expected we would take it hot, but he said: 'We will go first to pray in church.'

First things first! It's in little ways like this that Blessed Cyprian showed his endurance, his power to keep on doing the right thing even when human nature was crying out to take the easy line. Wouldn't *we* have excused ourselves and had the hot meal first?

On another occasion Michael Idigo recounts how he followed Cyprian to the church to pray. They recited the rosary, then the litany of the Blessed Virgin and the litany of the Sacred Heart. 'I was answering: *Ora pro nobis, ora pro n ...*' but fell asleep; then fell down, tired and hungry. 'Are you tired?' he asked me. 'Yes, sir,' I replied. 'Then go home to eat and sleep,' he said – continuing with his prayers. How like Our Lord who frequently went without sleep in order to pray and be with his Father.

Can you see from such examples the importance of endurance? Endurance means carrying on with our duties when it's uphill and difficult. It means doing things when not only human nature is rebelling, but everyone around is making it difficult. You just want to pack up and go home.

Jesus willingly put up with mental and physical agonies; and submitted to injustice, cruelty and pain. Why did he do this? Not merely out of obedience ('he was obedient to death on the cross'), but even deeper than that – out of *love*, love for me, love for you. This love spurred him on to suffer and to die to save us.

We have a further example of this in Blessed Cyprian's life. In July 1925, Michael Iwene announced his decision to go to the seminary. This was an extraordinary step for someone who came so recently from a pagan background. His family and friends were not only dismayed, they were utterly opposed to it. A cousin, Robert Oraekie, shouted at him: 'Shut up! You fool! You can't do this after all I have trained you for!' Michael Iwene stood his ground and meekly said, 'Thank you, sir', and walked away. The rest of the villagers shared Mr Oraekie's fears. Some even thought he was out of his mind. In spite of all these pressures and mounting opposition, Michael Iwene stood his ground. How blessed we are that he did!

Great men (and holy people!) must have endurance. They must be able to put up with long, hard years of training and self-discipline in the small things first, then in the great challenges of life. Can you put up with being too hot or too cold, with food which doesn't suit you, with things that go wrong (and they do)? Can you put up with being wrongly judged; can you stand the pinpricks of daily life? The pinpricks can be seen as such, or, there's another, better way of looking at them. You can look at them as splinters of a cross. For many of us, a whole cross would be too hard to bear; no, our cross is built up little by little; we are asked to endure a splinter at a time.

Then, simply *endure*. Endure the many things which go wrong each day – the burnt toast, the late bus, the angry workmate, the annoying jibe, the insult, the parking or speeding fine, the disappointments, your worries and your fears, the broken sleep, the noisy neighbours, the crowded tube, the lack of understanding – the weakness of yourself and others.

How can we show endurance? Basically by showing love, for 'love *endures* forever: love never ends'. Be patient with those over you, and kind to those under you. Be gentle with the old and the young, the sick and the overenthusiastic. Patience, gentleness and kindness: these are virtues to practise because they all require endurance.

If you want to know how to endure, you have a wonderful teacher before you in Blessed Cyprian. He endured so many things for the love of Our Lord. He teaches us so clearly that greatness, great holiness, isn't made up of success and dazzling achievements. Not for him the large crowd of followers, the brilliant preaching, books that sold by the thousand. Not for him a comfortable and cosy existence. He took all his hardships in his stride: the strides with which he followed Christ. It was from Christ that he drew the grace and strength to endure to the end. 'When I am weak, then I am strong.' 'By the grace of God, I am what I am.'

Blessed Cyprian help us and make us worthy of your example.

Stand up and be counted

St Clare's Pilgrimage (1978)

Our theme today ('stand up and be counted') is well chosen for those of you who are leaving St Clare's this term. As you grow older you gain more independence, you have to do more and more things for yourselves. This applies very much to your Catholic Faith. It will be more and more up to you. Have you ever seen the folk costumes different nationalities wear on big occasions to keep alive their national spirit? Poles, Czechs, Swiss. Very colourful and all that but keeping up one's faith is not a simple matter of putting on a folk costume from time to time and nothing else. It is a personal matter between Jesus and me even as it was for the two people we heard about in the readings. St Stephen was ready to be stoned to death not for the sake of his nation but for Jesus' sake. St Peter was too. His failure and denial of Our Lord the first time around was a warning to us of how hard it is going to be at times. St Peter repented not because he'd dirtied his Catholic folk costume but because he had let Jesus down. Turning one's back on the church is one thing; turning one's back on Jesus is another. That's what we are standing up for.

I was thinking that this group of you here is a good example of what the church is like and what it is trying to do. The church is like a group of musicians – an orchestra if you like – or any group of instrumentalists and vocalists.

As you know an instrument is basically a very simple piece of mechanism. A drum is a wooden box with two pieces of skin stretched across it at either end. A guitar is another sort of box with a long piece of wood attached to it and pieces of gut or wire stretched along it. A trumpet is a metal tube with a flared end. You can make a noise by blowing down any piece of pipe. Over the years these instruments have been improved upon.

In untrained and unpractised hands the noises that come out of them are simply awful. But given a bit of training more and more beautiful sounds can be produced.

Now, in an orchestra some instruments require more skill than others. Some instruments sound well as solo instruments, others are pretty pointless on their own. Again you may not have a lot of notes to play or you may have the lead role and be playing all the time. Playing the triangle is not as skilled as playing the violin but provided that that triangle plays its notes at the right time and the right place the piece of music is transformed.

Where is this leading us to? We are all playing an instrument in God's church. It may only be a triangle; it may be a key instrument like the piano. All God is asking us is to play our part.

What are we playing: an orchestra without music would be useless, wouldn't it? So God has given us some music to play: the song of salvation. Not to have something to sing about would have been as pointless as your coming here today with your guitars without having anything to sing. We want to sing about God's love for us, i.e. Jesus and our love for God through Jesus.

I've already mentioned how few instruments sound well on their own. A guitar is not up to much without the singers. The trumpet part of a concert wouldn't sound as well without the orchestra to back it up. So each of us, without the church, would be lost on our own. We might risk playing 'Three Blind Mice' or something, but nothing very great for fear of making a mistake. That's what happens when you try to manage without the church. Unless we belong to the church's orchestra and play the music composed by God and conducted by the Pope, we won't sound very well. But if we do, each of us will be able to do something beautiful for God and the sound of our music will spread about us. When others hear they will want to know who the composer was and who was conducting. But if you just play 'Three Blind Mice' on your own, no one will take any notice.

The final point is this. Just to play the right notes is not enough, you must put your heart into it otherwise it will be a very deadly thing. 'Happiness is where you are and what you want to be.' If you sing or play with all your skill and love that is the surest way of standing up properly and letting yourself be counted.

Dedication of the Church

(1996)

We are built up as living stones into the house and altar of God

Origen says

> All of us who believe in Christ Jesus are said to be *living stones* according to scripture where it says: 'Like *living stones* be yourselves built into a spiritual house, to be a holy priesthood, to offer spiritual sacrifices to God through Jesus Christ' (Rom 12:1).

We are *not only living stones* in the Church as a whole, but also in our own church at Mount Saint Bernard. This point is one we are familiar with from St Bernard's sermons. The feast of the Dedication of our church is our own special feast, and no one else will celebrate it if we don't. But he goes even further: It is still more our own because it is the feast of our own selves. This may embarrass you, but 'be not like horse and mule unintelligent, needing bridle and bit'. It does sound a bit exaggerated to call it a feast of this community. Yet, it is no more far-fetched than having a feast for a building of bricks and stones. Bernard says:

> These bricks and stones are undoubtedly holy, but it is because of your bodies … when this house was consecrated to the Lord by the ministry of the bishops, it was manifestly for our sakes it was done; and not just for those of us who were actually present at the time, but also for the sake of all those who until the end of time shall serve God in this place. Therefore, dearest brethren, it is necessary that what has already been accomplished in the walls in a visible manner should be invisibly fulfilled in ourselves (p. 388).

In his sermons for the Dedication he devotes a lot of time to comparing the labour and toil required to build the church with our labour and toil needed to conform ourselves into the likeness of Christ.

He also uses the different parts of the service of consecration to show how they symbolise what should be happening in our souls. The feast, then, is as much about us *living stones* as about the fabric of the church.

Caesarius of Arles puts it very succinctly:

The more profoundly we meditate on our salvation, the more deeply we come to realise that we are indeed the true and living temples of God. God does not live only in shrines made by man, structures of wood or stone, but above all he lives in the soul which is made after his image; shrines built by the hand of the great craftsman himself. St Paul's words are: 'God's temple is holy, and that temple you are (1 Cor 3:16–17)'.

In his second sermon, Bernard, to avoid the impression that the church itself is only of secondary importance, devotes his attention to the fact that the church is God's dwelling place. We need to have the external edifice of the church as much as we need the outward signs of the sacraments – both are symbols of God's presence and action in our souls.

Long ago a glorious king, none other than holy David, began to occupy his mind with a consideration full of piety. He judged it an unbecoming thing that the Lord God of Sabaoth had as yet no house upon earth ... My brethren, this is a matter which from us also demands some serious thought, yea, and high courage in translating thought into action.

Then Bernard gets sidetracked and for a while you are left wondering whether the *high courage in translating thought into action* isn't more about conversion than about building a church or temple.

In his sixth sermon Bernard does finally get around to speaking of the church as the dwelling place of God:

Jacob was a man, and once while asleep he saw the holy angels descending and ascending. But there is something more marvellous still. He testified that the Lord of angels was himself present also, for he said on awakening: 'Truly the Lord is in this place and I knew it not' (Gen 18:12).

Caesarius also shows the vital connection between the church and the soul:

God out of his kindness has made us into a dwelling-place for himself. If we want to celebrate the birthday of this church with true joy, we must not destroy the living temple of God within us by our sins. I shall put it in a way everybody can understand. Let your souls be as spotless and shining as you want this church to be when you come into it ... Just as you come in this church, so God wants to come into your soul, as he promised when he said; 'I will live in them and move among them.'

Yet, always the fathers come back to this fundamental dogma that *we* are the living stones in whom God loves to dwell. Origen who develops the idea of living stones, wants to know who are the foundation stones and finds the answer in St Paul: apostles and the prophets. He quotes Eph 2:20–22:

You are built upon the foundation of the apostles and prophets, Christ Jesus himself being the cornerstone. He is the one who holds the whole building together and makes it grow into a sacred temple dedicated to the Lord. In union with him you too (you and I) are being built together with all the others into a place where God lives through his Spirit.

This passage from Ephesians demonstrates that what the Fathers were teaching was already there in Paul. Origen adds:

But God cannot live in these living stones unless they are founded on the apostles and the prophets and have Christ for their corner stone. 'For no other foundation can anyone lay than that which is laid, Christ Jesus' (1 Cor 3:10ff). Blessed therefore are those who will be found to have constructed sacred and religious buildings upon that glorious foundation.

St Augustine, as you can imagine has something to say about this:

The festivity that has brought us together today is the dedication of the house of prayer. It is the house of our prayer, whilst we ourselves are the house of God. Now, if we are the house of God, we are being built up in this life and shall be consecrated at the last day. The work of building implies much labour, but the dedication shall be a time of jubilee. (He then explains how this building of us as houses of prayer takes place.) For, by believing, they are hewn, as it were, like wood and stones from the forests and mountains. And they are chipped, shaped, and smoothed under the hands of the tradesman whilst they are catechised, baptised, and formed in the faith. Nevertheless, it is only when they are bound together in charity that they constitute the house of God.

Charity is the cement which holds the building together. Notice how there is a change of emphasis, a change from simply building the dwelling to the cement needed to hold the stones together. St Augustine says:

> 'Thus had not these pieces of material wood and stone been united to each other in due order, had they not been firmly wedded to each other, did they not by their cohesion manifest their mutual love, so to speak, nobody would venture beneath them. But whenever you behold the wood and the stones in a building firmly fastened together you enter the building with confidence and have no fear of its falling' [St Bernard uses the psalm to make it more graphic]: Christ will not enter where there is a tottering wall or a tumbling fence (p. 397).

But, St Bernard won't let us forget that unless the members of the church are united – held together by the love of Christ, individual holiness is of no value. Taking a phrase of Isaiah (out of context) 'The solder is good', he says:

> There is in fact a twofold solder cementing these living stones, the solder of full knowledge and the solder of perfect love. For the more intimate is their union with him who is love (quoting St John's God is love, 1 Jn 4:16) the more powerful must be the bonds of love that unite them one with another ... Wood and stones do not constitute a house so long as they remain disunited, nor is it possible to dwell beneath them until they have been cemented together: it is only in combination that they can form a dwelling place.

'When two or three are gathered together in Christ's name is he there in their midst.' Only where love is present is God present, for 'God is love' (1 Jn 4:16).

The Feast of the Dedication of the church is the celebration of a symbol. It celebrates the completion of the labours and effort gone into building a house for God and the joyous occasion when it was finally finished and consecrated. All this is but a symbol of the labour and effort that has to be put into building the living stones into temples fit for God to dwell in. It's an ongoing process, which as yet is incomplete. But hopefully, one day, it will be finished and we will be ready not just for God to dwell in us but for us to be with God.

CLOSING PRAYER

Lord God you choose men as living stones to become an eternal dwelling, built to the glory of your name. Increase your gifts of grace to the Church, and let your faithful people throng in ever greater numbers to form the heavenly Jerusalem.

Thanksgiving

(1981)

This is a season of harvest and thanksgiving festivals; it is a time of looking back over the summer and recalling some of the highlights. The purpose I have in mind is to deepen our conviction of the value of God's gifts and to be more grateful. 'What have you that you have not received?' St Paul asks. And not only have we received all the good things in life, we in no way deserved them. It's so vital that we should become more aware, deep down, of the personal and loving care God has for each of us. Without this fundamental disposition of gratitude our faith is a dead loss.

A story I read recently will serve to bring out this basic ingredient of all goodness and happiness. A lady came to Fr Bernard Häring and told him about the desperate state of her family life. Her husband had given up all care for their children and allowed them to go their own sweet way – with the inevitable consequences. They were getting more and more unmanageable. Fr Häring's advice was simple.

> Take time out every evening to thank God for all he has given you, for his providence in giving a home and security, and healthy children. By degrees, invite the children to join you in this act of thanksgiving. Finally, prevail upon your husband to join this family prayer of thanksgiving.

Well, after, six months the lady returned to Fr Häring and told him how things had gone. The family had been transformed. 'Now, I realise,' she said to him, 'the value of thanks and how we must praise God for all his gifts. When we cease to thank God, *our* faith dies.'

'When you cease to thank God, *your* faith dies.' Doesn't this come very near to explaining why the faith of so many people today has grown cold? We live in a society that has never had it so good. The only fault of many parents is that they have been too generous, too unsparing of themselves, with the result their children have grown up taking it all for granted. What their parents didn't give them or do for them the State supplied. They may have been told to say 'thank you', but it was a mere formula. They never learned to see gifts as wholly undeserved and unmerited. Rather, they came to look upon them as their just deserts, something they had a right to. So they never knew what it meant to be grateful, to have a grateful heart. 'When you cease to give thanks, *your* faith dies.'

And now I come to think of it, isn't there quite a bit about thanking in the gospels? One of Jesus' most frequent phrases is 'I thank you Father.' He did so before every great miracle – the raising of Lazarus, for example. He did it before the miracle of miracles – the changing of bread and wine into his body and blood.

Ingratitude was one of the things that surprised Our Lord. 'Weren't ten made whole? Where are the other nine? Was there no one to return arid give thanks to God except this foreigner?' (17:17–18) It was particularly galling to find it was the people of his own household who had taken it for granted and not come back to say thank you.

St Paul's letters return time and time again to the need to be thankful. 'Be happy at all times; pray constantly and for all things give thanks to God because this is what God expects you to do in Christ Jesus.' (1 Thess 5:18) 'Always be *thankful* ... with gratitude in your hearts sing psalms and hymns and inspired songs to God ... giving thanks to God the Father through Christ' (Col 3:16, cf. 4:2).

Through Christ – the word Eucharistia means giving thanks. It became a key word in the New Testament, describing our first response to the wonderful things God has done for us in Christ. Jesus is our thanksgiving. He gave thanks to the Father through his saving death. And now we do the same: 'Through him, with him, in him.' Once we cease to offer the Mass, the *Eucharist*, our faith dies.

It is worth mentioning, by way of a final point, that, although our first reason for showing our gratitude to God through Christ is to express our awareness of how totally unworthy and undeserving we are of all his good gifts; Failure to be thankful places a major obstacle to God's generosity in the future. It's only natural: you don't go on giving to someone who doesn't show the slightest gratitude. St Teresa of Avila says, 'People will cry out, "God has forgotten me. He is deaf to my prayers".' But isn't the reason their failure to thank? They have taken God for granted and expected his gifts as their due. When we cease to thank God, *our* faith dies.

Let me close with a short quotation from St Augustine: 'Thanks be to God – what better words to shape our minds, or fit our tongue, or grace our pen? No prayer is shorter to say, sweeter to hear, grander to think on, or more fruitful to practise.'

Let us bless the Lord – Thanks be to God